The Harlots of Haverstock Hill

George II, Portrait by Thomas Hudson, 1744, during whose reign the events in this book unfurl.
Born in 1683, Prince of Wales from 1714 and King of Great Britain and Ireland from 1727 until his death in 1760.

The Harlots of Haverstock Hill

'Moll' King and her Belsize Houses

David S. Percy

λ
Aulis Publishers
London

The Harlots of Haverstock Hill

Present day photographs David S. Percy
Archive images Public Domain or Creative Commons licences
except where indicated.

Cover image *Young Woman at her Toilette*
Niklas Lafrensen *c.*1780.

Aulis Publishers
1 Belsize Avenue
London NW3 4BL UK
belsizevillage.co.uk

British Library Cataloguing-in-Publication Data.
A catalogue record of this book is available from the British Library.

ISBN 978-1-898541-21-9

Printed and bound by SRP Ltd Exeter UK

In memory of the earliest settlers in Belsize Park.

Contents

Foreword

This is an important book because it gives substance to one of the legends of Georgian London and brings to life one of the city's more fascinating and enigmatic characters. The legend has to do with the role the sex industry played in the building of Georgian London. The city's domestic architecture was, from the late 17th century and well into the 19th, largely the creation of speculating builders. But where did the money come from that enabled these builders to invest so extensively in the often very stylish expansion of the capital?

At the time London had many valuable trades and industries but, arguably, one of the most valuable was its sex industry. This perhaps surprising contention is based on contemporary evidence. Admittedly much of this is circumstantial, often little better than hearsay – it must be remembered that objectively or scientifically gathered statistics was a Victorian innovation. But there is a consistency of opinion, much of it seemingly informed, that asserts the startling fact – accepted at the time – that in London one woman in five was involved in the capital's sex industry. This was stated by the author of the *Congratulatory Epistle of a Reformed Rake*, published in 1758, who claimed that 'according to ... calculation ... there are Sixty-two Thousand, Five Hundred Whores' in London. This view was more or less supported in the late 1780s by a most observant foreign visitor, Johann Wilhelm von Archenholtz, who observed in his journal that 'London is said to contain fifty thousand prostitutes, without reckoning kept mistresses.' Which is to say 50,000 full-time prostitutes.

A similar – and far more authoritative – estimate was made in 1795 by the police magistrate Patrick Colquhoun at a time when London's population was around 730,000 meaning that, if a third were women of sexually active age, then indeed about one woman in five was involved in one way or the other with the sex industry in late 18th century London. If that was the case, then the industry was vast and the profits it made were huge.

One of the more memorable characters involved in this industry was Moll King. Her story is complex, indeed contemporary records suggest that there were several Moll Kings operating almost simultaneously within London's sex industry or criminal underworld. One of these Moll Kings was an associate of 'thief-taker' and gangster Jonathan Wilde, and was probably the inspiration for Daniel Defoe's novel *Moll Flanders*. The best known is the Moll King that, with her husband Tom, kept a coffee shop in the piazza in Covent Garden that appears in Hogarth's 1736 painting of the piazza and is referred to in numerous contemporary accounts which make it clear that Moll was part of the sex industry and that her coffee shop was essentially a bawdy house.

This is the Moll King followed in this book and what is particularly interesting is that her tale suggests how a proportion of the money generated by the sex industry was invested – or to use a modern term 'laundered' – through speculative house construction. Her story is told here in the form of an 18th century autobiography. This is picturesque and appropriate since so many of the sex industry's leading ladies – many in their day courted as celebrities – were commemorated through spicy autobiographies and biographies aimed at the popular market. Indeed Moll King was commemorated by such a publication, *The Life and Character of Moll King, Late Mistress of King's Coffee House in Covent Garden,* that appeared soon after her death in 1747. This anonymously authored publication makes it clear that Moll was successful in her various enterprises because in the 1730s she was able to purchase 'an estate' on Haverstock Hill, Hampstead where she built herself 'a very genteel County-House.' This is confirmed by a curious 1779 publication entitled *Nocturnal Revels* which states that Moll 'built a row of houses in the road near Hampstead' and by Moll King's own will which records that she owned properties in Hampstead.

This book tells the story of this building enterprise in unprecedented and riveting detail, with the site of Moll King's own house and its surviving adjoining 'villa' being identified and with evidence collected to suggest that some of these houses functioned as discrete extramural bordellos. The final section of this book is a splendid detective story and concludes with an important discovery because it helps to sustain the speculation that the 18th century sex industry spread its tentacles wide and did indeed make a substantial contribution to the construction of Georgian London.

Dan Cruickshank, April 2020

Dan Cruickshank is the author of
The Secret History of Georgian London: How the Wages of Sin Shaped the Capital
Random House, 2009

Preface

I chose to write about the main character in this book because she was one of the earliest settlers on Haverstock Hill, which is close to where I live. Her story began to fascinate me after discovering an old engraving that depicts a charming view from a house, belonging to a woman called Moll King, looking across open fields towards London.

Moll King, born in 1696 in conditions of extreme poverty, became during the course of the early 18th century a woman of means and property, dying at the age of 51 in one of three substantial houses she owned on Haverstock Hill, the road leading from London to Hampstead.

I have, in examining the various accounts of her life, together with evidence to be found on present-day Haverstock Hill, come to the conclusion that she chose that locality for very specific reasons. Some aspects of that conclusion are, I admit, conjectural. So I have elected to tell Moll's story in the form of an autobiography she never wrote – but plausibly could have done. Nevertheless, all the events, places, timings and names of individuals in her story are real.

Maps, illustrations, relevant images and photographs, together with supporting notes, have been added to the text.

David S. Percy
London, May 2020

A few introductory background notes

Prostitution in the 18th century was one of the few ways in which a woman might make a living, and those who chose, or were forced into this trade fell into three main categories. The lowliest were the streetwalkers while at the other extreme were the fashionable, superior brothels. At the high-end of the business there were courtesans, also called demi-reps; mistresses maintained by wealthy individuals who provided accommodation, fine clothes and jewellery.

Between the streetwalkers and the courtesans were those who lived and worked in bagnios and brothels. A bagnio was a bathhouse, some actually did offer bathing facilities, but many were essentially little more than bawdy-houses, offering sexual services. These bawdy-houses, along with the brothels, most of which at that time were in Covent Garden or Soho, were run by women known as mothers. Women like Moll King.

Young girls born into poverty were considered fortunate if they were employed in bawdy-houses, where they were firmly controlled. On joining a bagnio or brothel new girls had their clothes and personal belongings taken away. This was generally the case no matter how they had been discovered or where they were from. They would be charged for their lodgings and, during the first half of the 18th century, each girl's earnings would just about cover the costs of her rent and food, a system that meant the girls were trapped by their keepers. Day clothes were provided, with the appropriate dress for seducing clients and, especially in the evenings and at night, their wardrobe would correspond with the client's preferences. For important occasions the client's fees would be adjusted to cover the expense of hiring special dresses, hats and accessories.

Section of Rocque's sixteen-sheet map of London and its environs published in 1746, with the route between Covent Garden and Belsize in added colour, as surveyed and drawn by John Rocque Land Surveyor; & Engraved by Richard Parr.

Moll King's Story

1. 'Moll' King, behind her counter pouring liquor into a small glass, etching and engraving, printmaker anonymous, *c.*1740.
According to a biographical pamphlet published shortly after her death in 1747, *The Life and Character of Moll King*, she was a prostitute in her early teens.

2. Vine Street, renamed Grape Street, was in the parish of St. Giles-in-the-Fields, the building is depicted here as it was during Moll's time in 1718. This was the second church of St. Giles built on this site. Following the Great Fire of London in 1666 there was a massive increase in property building. In 1685 there were about two thousand registered houses in the parish, and by 1715 there were over three thousand.

CHAPTER 1

Humble Beginnings

Let me introduce myself. My name is Moll King and mine is no ordinary tale. I was low-born, but unlike so many poor wretches around me I rose above my humble beginnings to become a woman of means. A woman to whom others paid respect and who took charge of her destiny. Mine is a tale of opportunities spied and grasped, of intrigue and artifice and of revels and revelations. Along the way I encountered those, from common street beggars to exalted nobles, who both hindered and helped me in my quest to move up in the world.

My start in life was a harsh one. I was born in the year 1696 in a comfortless garret in a poor dwelling in Vine Street, St. Giles-in-the-Fields, London. My father was a shoemaker, a respectable trade, although not a lucrative one. He had his own place of work as a chamber-master, while my mother sold fruit, fish and vegetables from a barrow. They named me Mary, as was recorded on a number of documents – I became Moll later in life for reasons which will become obvious.

My father, occupied as he was with his work, had little time for me, but my mother took me with her into the bustling streets of Covent Garden where she plied her trade and taught me the value of hard work.

Mary King's signature.

3. Part of Covent Garden Piazza, Pieter Angillis, *c.*1726, Yale Centre for British Art, Paul Mellon Collection. The 4th Earl of Bedford commissioned Inigo Jones to build the residential square, which Jones designed along the lines of the piazza of Livorno, Italy – the first regularly planned square in London.

Many who were from humble beginnings like mine lived desperate and hopeless lives. But I wanted none of that, I vowed that I would do better and take advantage of any opportunities that presented themselves to me. I observed those who were better off and determined to break loose from my birthright and to use the natural guile and commonsense I possessed to improve my lot in life.

At fourteen years of age I was sent into domestic service in a well-to-do household in the Strand. However, life working as a lowly servant, under an unforgiving master and mistress, was not for me. On cold, cheerless nights sleeping in the kitchen after long days of unremitting hard work, I pictured myself one day living in a country house with servants of my own. How I would manage that, coming from nothing and possessing nothing, I did not know. But if my resolve and strong will would suffice, I would find a way.

The education in housekeeping that I received while in service was to be of use to me later, but my intent was to remain for as short a time as possible with my employers. As soon as I could I left them and vowed to follow in my mother's footsteps.

Covent Garden Market in those days was a scruffy, busy place, filled with a throng of people, some selling, some buying, and some there simply to enjoy parading around the market and making eyes at others in the crowd. The market was held within a grand square, a vast Italian-style piazza designed by the famous Inigo Jones, but the traders had soon arrived and covered its clean lines and gravel floors with the filth of rotting food and flowers. Only on Sundays and Christmas Day was the hue and cry of the market silent.

I loved the market, with its noise and vibrancy. Filled with stalls, shops and sheds selling all manner of fruits, vegetables, roots, herbs and flowers. It was a lively, intriguing place for a young girl to work – although smelly at times! I sold from a barrow, rising in darkness in the early hours of the morning to purchase my stock of fruit and sometimes green vegetables from the growers who brought their crops to the city in carts overnight.

It was said of me that I was tolerably handsome, jolly and sprightly, with good natural sense. I had a winning smile and a way with words and I sold my wares to all who came, from kitchen maids to lords and ladies.

4. The celebrated Sally Salisbury, 18th-century courtesan, well dressed, well connected and renowned for her beauty and witty repartee.

KING 1707–13.
Thomas, *b.* at West Ashton, Wilts; admitted K.S. 1708, aged about 14; admitted scholar at King's College, Cambridge, 2 Dec. 1713; his place there seems to have been filled up in Nov. 1716, when he left in apprehension that his fellowship would be denied him; kept a coffee-house in Covent Garden, which was called after him; his widow, 'Moll' King—a very disreputable person—continued the coffee-house after his death. (*Eton Coll. Reg.;* Austin Dobson, *Eighteenth Century Vignettes* (1907), 3rd Ser., p. 345.)

5. Eton College Register entry for Thomas King. Tom was born in Wiltshire in 1694, from a reasonably well-to-do family and they were able to send young Thomas King to Eton College. Records in the Eton archive confirm that he attended Eton from 1707-1713. Thomas was admitted as a King's Scholar to King's College Cambridge, but he apparently dropped out by 1716. This no doubt disappointed his parents.

The market could be a dangerous place. Thieves, pick-pockets, beggars and wretches of every description lurked there and brawls between toss pots (drunkards) fresh from the taverns were commonplace. Harlots and strumpets in fancy dresses paraded the streets, showing off their wares to the gentlemen who passed by. Young girls wandering alone were often snared by the bawds who ran the punch-houses (brothels), always on the look out for fresh young prey for the rakes who frequented their premises.

As time passed I became well known in the market and I was able to count many, from all walks of life, among my friends and acquaintances. One day I encountered Nanny Cotton, a noted courtesan and companion of the beautiful Sally Salisbury. Sally was Mother Elizabeth Wisebourne's best girl (later in Mother Needham's household) and she had become a celebrated harlot and the lover of many notable members of society and patrons of wealth, including some say, the Prince of Wales. Nanny and I became acquainted and she offered to help me by lending me a generous sum of money on favourable terms.

With this loan and Nanny Cotton's introductions I was able to improve my offerings. I began to increase my takings and was soon able to repay her. My situation became even more advantageous after I decided to specialise in the sale of nuts. I purchased wholesale and by dint of working long hours and being always ready with a saucy smile for the gentlemen who passed by, my business grew considerably.

By this time I had exchanged my barrow for a stall and soon afterwards I met a young man by the name of Thomas King. Tom and I came from different worlds. He was well-born and had been educated at Eton College and at King's College in Cambridge University. But he had left his studies under a cloud after some misdeed and no longer mixed with the great and the good who had once been his companions. Tom took what work he could find in Covent Garden and it was there that we met. I found him good company and in 1717, when I was 21 and he was 23, we were married secretly, or rather 'tack'd together'. Marriages like ours, in the locality of the Fleet Prison, were so called in part because the banns had not been read and in part owing to some kind of legal quirk which meant that members of the clergy conducting marriages in that environ could not be prosecuted. But while ours may not

6. Typical clandestine Fleet wedding (prior to the Marriage Act coming into force in 1754).

have been an official marriage, for me and Tom it was real enough.

It is said that around this time I was supplementing the earnings from my stall through the art of pick-pocketing. There were well-known thieves and deceivers who had many, young and old, working for them, all well-trained in the necessary skills of removing a snuff box or gold watch from the pocket of a wealthy man. It has been written that I was among them and was caught, and that the acclaimed author Daniel Defoe visited me in the vile prison known as Newgate Gaol to record my story in his notebook. On this subject I have little to say. If 'twas me, then I found a way to slip the bonds of imprisonment and return to the streets, but I am confessing to naught; there were many young women with the same name as mine at that time, and surely it was another who had such an encounter.

I had learned early on the advantage to be had from the right social connections. Nanny Cotton taught me well. Her companion Sally had been a street prostitute who rose to become the most famous courtesan in the land; she dressed in fine silks and mixed with nobles. Heeding her example, I made sure to cultivate friends of the right sort wherever I went.

After a few years of marriage to Tom I was drawn into a liaison with a charming fellow named Murray who held a high position in one of the public offices. We were together for some time, during which he introduced me to a number of influential and well-connected people in whose good favour I took pains to remain.

Gossips had it that this affair was more to do with seeking advantage on my part, than with a true softening of the heart, but I like to think that it was a little of both. After Murray and I parted ways and I had entertained a few other minor dalliances, I returned to my husband Tom, who welcomed me back. During my absence he had taken employment as a waiter in a bawdy-house in Covent Garden and his experience in this position was to benefit us.

Now was the time to start implementing a plan I had long held dear. When I suggested to Tom that we set up in business together, he readily fell in with the idea. Using the money saved from my profitable fruit and nut stall, we were now in a position to advance ourselves. Tom and I had a good understanding of one another and what each of us might contribute to our business venture.

7. The church of St. Paul, Covent Garden after Thomas Girtin, Tate Images. Attributed to Inigo Jones and completed in 1633 the building follows Vitruvius's design for a Tuscan temple – the first authentically classical church built in England.

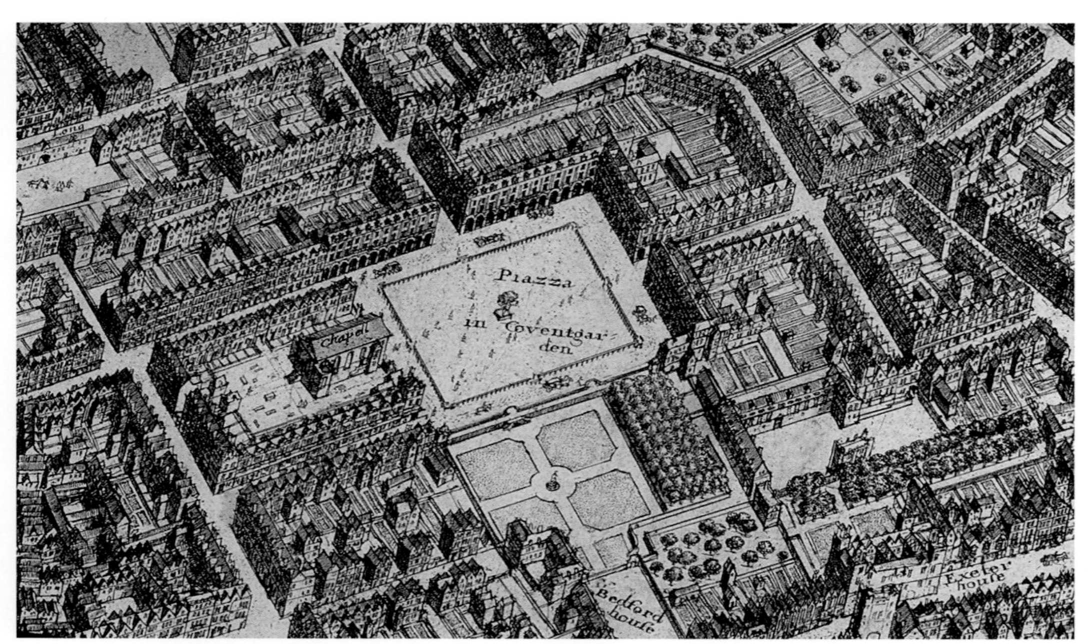

8. Bird's-eye plan of the west central district of London centred on Covent Garden, etching detail, Wenceslaus Hollar, *c*.1660. Laid out as an Italian-style piazza, the piazza is drawn here as it was originally, gravelled, with a fence all round it and a tree in the centre. The terraced houses to the south of Russell Street (the smaller square) were known as the Little Piazza and the grand houses in the north of the square were referred to as the Great Piazza.

Tom brought his education and social standing, along with his ready conviviality, while for my part I brought a quick wit, a good head for figures and steady judgment in matters of business.

By the early 1720s Tom and I had opened our first enterprise together. We both knew that a shared coffee-house business would be the ideal way to advance our fortunes so we rented from the Duke of Bedford, the leaseholder of Covent Garden, a small shack erected on part of the piazza at £12 per annum. Rudimentary and mostly constructed of wood, it was simple inside and out and from it we began to serve coffee, tea and chocolate to the market people at a penny a dish. London water being virtually undrinkable, coffee was fast gaining in popularity as an alternative to beer or liquor for those who wanted to remain clear-headed.

We called our establishment King's Coffee House – a grander title than was merited by our modest premises, but nonetheless a good one. Knowing of Tom's earlier abrupt departure from university, our wittier clients often referred to it as 'King's College'. Well, it was certainly the source of much education, as you shall shortly discover.

9. Covent Garden Piazza looking north, from an engraving by Sutton Nicholls, *c.*1720, first published in *London Described* in 1731. St. Paul's Church is on the left. Initially King's Coffee House was located in one of the three sheds in the foreground. Until the arrival of coffee-houses, the only places available to meet up with friends to enjoy a drink or two and engage in intellectual discussion of anything and everything from literature to philosophy, were the established public houses or taverns.

Despite the bustle of the busy market in the piazza and the growing number of traders and visitors, the area benefited considerably from the wider streets than those of the City. The streets in the area could easily accommodate carriages, which encouraged wealthy shoppers to visit the clothiers and drapers located in Covent Garden.

CHAPTER 2

Covent Garden & the Coffee House

Covent Garden was at that time one of the largest, most successful and best known markets in the city. In addition to the buying and selling of fish, nuts, fruit and vegetables there were the coffee-houses and taverns, plus of course the punch-houses and the street girls. All came there; high and low born, wealthy and poor, old and young. They came for business and for pleasure or simply to gawp at others.

Our coffee-house was situated in an excellent position on the south side of the market, just a short distance from St. Paul's Church. From the start the business thrived. We remained open in the early hours of the morning to accommodate the marketeers who came to buy and sell goods, as well as the misses and young rakes who arranged to meet there for the pursuance of nocturnal intrigues.

I wanted our establishment to differ from the usual run of Covent Garden taverns and in this we succeeded. For those from all walks of life we provided what the taverns could not and, as word spread that Kings was open for business through the night, visitors soon flocked to fill the place and within a short time ours had become a well known 'night-house'.

As the business grew we leased two more adjoining sheds. Even with the additional space we scarcely had sufficient room for all our customers. And what customers we had!

They came to partake, to gossip and to flirt and included among their number not only the market traders, porters and wenches, but gentlemen of fashion and some of the gayest and brightest ladies of the town. On occasion we even hosted noblemen in full dress and ladies in fine silks, all of them rubbing shoulders with the common market folk.

The sheds we leased were flimsy and they provided the most basic of shelters, open to the winds and liable to collapse, but despite their miserable appearance I put great care into the arrangements within.

Our largest shed we named the Long Room and within it we positioned six benches with upright backs, each wide enough for two persons and in addition eight smaller tables and two flap tables alongside benches and wooden stools, all of which were placed around the stove grate which was always filled with a merrie fire to warm away the night chill.

The two smaller rooms were furnished with tables and chairs and each heated by a stove grate. To complete the furnishings, and to shut out prying eyes, I placed curtains across the small openings that served for windows.

We added makeshift bedchambers above the rooms of the coffee-house, accessed by a ladder that could be drawn up and stowed away. The two wooden bedsteads in the sleeping quarters had feather beds with bolsters and blankets, a chest of drawers, with a couple of rugs covering the floor.

Behind the public rooms lay a kitchen which while crude in its construction, was still equipped with a large supply of punch bowls, coffee and chocolate cups. Here we also kept our stock of beer, ale and strong liquors, including plenty of diddle (gin) for those with a taste for more than mere coffee.

I was proud of how well-equipped our place was. The sheds survived for some time, despite their somewhat rickety appearance, and over the years that followed they were reinforced and then rebuilt into more permanent structures. In the front we opened a shop, equipped with five cupboards with shelves, a counter for serving drinks, a selection of one-gallon pewter pots, decanters of all sizes and five dozen or so drinking glasses. In this manner customers with little time or inclination to come within to sit a while could take a drink before going on their way. And sometimes even those who were merely passing by for a quick sup could still be tempted to come inside for some good-time pleasures with our buxom girls.

10. Inside the busy King's Coffee House salon looking through to the shop or bar area to the piazza beyond, detail from an etching by George Bickham the Younger, *c.*1735, Trustees of the British Museum. King's offered brandy, arrack, and punch amongst their range of liquors.

Here drunken Templars, Rakes & Men of Taste:
Their Constitutions & their Substance waste –
Here lustful Strumpets with their Bosoms bare
Mix with a Motley Throng, drink, smoke & swear.

10a. By the early 18th century wooden bedsteads were becoming simpler in style, although many continued to be surrounded by heavy curtains. Cotton-filled mattresses were replacing hay, but still suspended by straps or ropes.

11. *Covent Garden Market and St. Paul's*, Balthazar Nebot, 1737, Tate Images. Covent Garden Piazza looking towards the church of St. Paul. The King's Coffee House was located in three of the single storey sheds on the left.

12. Market Girl, detail from *Covent Garden,* Pieter Angillis, *c.*1720, Google Art Project.

Those who did venture inside our coffee-house were greeted warmly by Black Betty, a hardworking woman who was with us for many years. Known by some as Tawny Betty, she was much admired for her calm and cheerful disposition and she kept an eye on the comely young women who served our customers their drinks with the sauciest of smiles and a wink that promised greater enjoyments to come.

I oversaw the comings and goings in our establishment with a gimlet eye – nothing passed me by and all those who were in our employ knew their place. While Tom entertained our customers with tall tales and mirth and drank along with them, I remained sober, forgoing alcohol in favour of a clear head in order to ensure that all was as it should be.

As might be expected, there were frequent attempts to put a stop to what some described as 'disgraceful goings-on' in our establishment. Many of the coffee-houses, including King's, acquired a reputation for instigating lascivious behaviour and general bad conduct. But none of this seemed to affect our business. Indeed, it appeared only to encourage it.

Inevitably, there was much over-indulgence, and those who were mauled (exceedingly drunk) and unable to get home, would be escorted by one of my cinder-garblers (female servants) with a lanthorn and candle to the bagnios located around the area. These Turkish bathhouses were comfortable, well-furnished places of pleasure; brothels with private rooms, offering fleshly services of all description, many remaining open all through the night.

In 1728 I gave birth to my only son, Charles, born on July 14 and christened in St. Martin-in-the-Fields on August 4. He was a bonny, charming baby beloved by us both, and we paid no heed to the gossips who questioned his paternity. Tom gave him the name King, and that was the end of the matter.

Hungry for ever greater success, I sought to develop further the business of running a discreet house of civil reception within our premises. I had learned well from Nanny and Sally and the other leading courtesans I encountered in my early days in the market and was determined that mine would be a high-class place offering only the cleanest girls, all of them pleasing, shapely and well-apparelled, appearing as courtesans of quality. No strumpets or dashers (showy harlots) for me, I encouraged girls who

13. *Covent Garden Piazza and Market*, detail, Samuel Scott, *c.*1755, Museum of London, Bridgeman Images. By the mid 18th century more sheds had been added to the piazza and other buildings benefited from additional height.

When in full swing the market was a cacophony of vendors proclaiming their wares. Women screaming and selling their fruit, stall holders bartering and haggling; the racket of rattling carts and barrows trundling to and from stalls, barrows and basket setups. There were sounds of horses, donkeys, knife grinders and noisy children. At the end of the morning this part of London smelled of fish, rotting fruit and vegetables.

were willing to work hard and who wished to do well and learn how to please our customers' every desire. I wished all comers, from the highest to the lowest to find a luscious nymph in waiting for them at my house.

This line of business earned me the name Moll, like so many others in the same trade. Not that I serviced the customers myself. I had dabbled in that business when I was younger, and had already taken a number of 'sweethearts' by the time I was fourteen years of age, but at King's I was interested solely in the managing of my girls who, as was only just, handed me their earnings as payment for the use of my premises and for the clothing and food I provided.

Many young girls plying their trade as harlots came asking me for loans to buy clothing and I did lend them money, as Sally's friend Nanny had once done for me. I knew that young girls struggled to earn a living in any other way and that the flesh trade was often their only choice. Indeed, at least one girl in every five worked in this trade at that time, either on the streets or between the sheets in a punch-house. So I was willing to help those who I judged would use my money to better themselves and not squander it on drink or worthless pastimes. I did, of course, expect to be repaid promptly, with considerable interest charged on the sum loaned, and any who thought they could swindle me soon learned otherwise.

While my stable of girls offered a variety of carnal services to those whose tastes ran to the bawdy, I was careful to avoid the charge of keeping a brothel by insisting that all services were to be provided *away from* the premises. The rooms above the shop were for family only, as I assured any visiting constables or justices. We also kept another room over in Hart Street which, I informed those same justices, was a family refuge for when the coffee-house became too rowdy.

With these precautions in place the most we could be accused of was running a disorderly house, a charge resulting in a modest fine, unlike the far more serious charge of running a bawdy-house.

I was one of a number of molls or bawds in the area. Old Betty Careless had a successful bagnio in the Little Piazza while, as a leading procuress, Mother Elizabeth Needham ran a very exclusive business in St. James's, servicing the most fashionable clients from the upper echelons of society.

14. *A Harlot's Progress,* plate 1, engraving detail, William Hogarth, 1732, later partial hand colour. A young girl, freshly arrived in London, is received by renowned procuress and brothel keeper Mother Needham on the right.

15. *A St. Giles's Beauty*, mezzotint with hand colour, printed for and sold by Carington Bowles, Trustees of the British Museum. Note the simple turn-up bedstead behind the curtain.

Artist William Hogarth, who became an acquaintance of mine, depicted her in one of his 1731 paintings entitled *A Harlot's Progress.*

Tragically the heartless Justice of the Peace John Gonson arrested her and she was sentenced to stand in the pillory (a wooden framework with holes for the head and hands) at Park Place in May, 1731. Poor Elizabeth was pelted to such an extent with all manner of vile items that after a few days she died of her injuries. A fate that made every one of us shiver with horror.

Some years later, in 1741, Mother Jane Douglas took over the *King's Head* tavern and she became very well known as was Mother Haywood, who used to pay me visits from her bagnio in Charles Street. We were in fierce competition with one another so we both maintained an especially close eye on our girls. And of course there was Haddock's Bagnio (figure 16), a large and successful brothel which, from around 1742, was located close to us on the northern side of the Great Piazza.

By then I was residing in Covent Garden only part of the time, as I shall shortly explain, but when I was at King's I would meet with the other bawds, inviting them to my place to sup and exchange gossip. Every one of us was on the look out for new talent to enhance our businesses, but if any of them eyed one of my girls with a view to snatching her away, as sometimes happened, I applied all the rules of commerce I had learned from buying and selling in the market.

We all kept our most valuable young girls, those yet to bed a man for the first time, close by us. They were an asset and a bargaining tool, attracting substantial payments from wealthy clients, many of whom believed that conjugation with a very young girl would cure them of the pox. A foolish and ill-informed but nonetheless useful notion.

I took pleasure in knowing that ours was among the most notorious – and the most popular of the coffee-houses. In 1730 a slim volume entitled *A Brief and Merrie History of England* was published. It was penned by that well-known satirist Anthony Hilliard, who wrote:

> They [Londoners] represent these Coffee-houses as the most agreeable Things in London ... but in other respects they are full of Smoak, like a Guard-Room.

16. *Covent Garden Piazza and Market*, detail, Samuel Scott, *c.*1755, Museum of London, Bridgeman Images. Haddock's Bagnio is located in the right foreground, No.8 Great Piazza, a carriage stands at the entrance. The brothel owned by Mother Douglas is in the next building.

17. Typical scene in an early 1700s London coffee-house, Bridgeman Images. The new houses became fashionable places for the chattering classes to meet, to conduct business, gossip, exchange ideas, and debate the news of the day. Londoners saw publication of the daily *London Courant* in the early 1700s, distributed to coffee-houses by runners bringing important updates or 'news 'flashes'.

This was followed by the *Review*, forerunner of the *Tatler* and then *The Spectator*. Several great British institutions can trace their roots back to the early coffee-houses. The London Stock Exchange had its beginnings in Jonathan's Coffee House in 1698. Auctions in salesrooms attached to coffee-houses were the beginnings of the auction houses of Sotheby's and Christies. Lloyd's of London has its origins in Lloyd's Coffee House founded on Tower Street in 1686, relocating five years later to Lombard Street.

18. *A Fool and his MONEY's soon PARTED the old booby half muzzy to a bagnio reel'd*, 1790. Stealing from customers by picking their pockets supplemented some workers' earnings.
But not all molls or ladies of pleasure did that sort of thing, and numerous terms were adopted to distinguish between regular harlots and those in the business who also resorted to stealing from their customers.

Anthony Hilliard continued,

> I believe 'tis these Places that furnish the Inhabitants with Slander, for there one hears exact Accounts of everything done in Town as if it were but a Village. At those Coffee-houses near the Court, called White's, St James', Williams's, the conversation turns chiefly upon Equipages, Essence, Horse-Matches, Tupees, Modes, Mortgages and Maidenheads; the Cocoa Tree upon Bribery and Corruption, Evil-Ministers, Errors and Mistakes in Government.

I laughed when I was read this, because he wrote the pure truth; our place was a hotbed of gossip and intrigue. Many came there to hear or exchange titbits of information about the comings and goings, financial affairs and scandalous liaisons of others, especially those of high-repute. There was slander aplenty, whispered behind gloved hands or into willing ears. I enjoyed the tales and did my fair share of passing them on; although I took care that none involved me or my business.

The garnering of intelligences was something at which Tom and I excelled. We had soon learned that coffee-house talk was a valuable commodity. Our house was all very open and so holding private conversations was extremely difficult. It was easy to overhear private exchanges, to ask seemingly innocent questions, to pry without appearing to pry, and to extract information from a customer who was groggified (tipsy) or too full of his own importance to know when to keep his mouth shut.

From our early days in Covent Garden we had cultivated the art of trading knowledge concerning all manner of business transactions. The right piece of intelligence could be worth a pretty penny when sold to an eager recipient and in this way we were able to increase our fortunes considerably.

I also taught my girls to pass on to me any information revealed by their culls (customers) in intimate moments. Many a customer unwittingly let slip details which could be traded for goods, favours or cash. But while I encouraged artful pillow-talk, I drew the line at extortion. It was not uncommon for working girls to demand payment from their customers on the pretext of being with child. To avoid embarrassment and a potential ruinous outcome, the client could be tricked into handing over a considerable sum.

Some molls spurred their girls to involve themselves in this kind of racket, and even acted as go-between, but I had no stomach for such crude goings-on. And besides, Tom and I did well enough with the coffee-house business, the girls and the sale of information.

The attractions of the market were enhanced threefold when the Covent Garden Theatre opened its doors for the first time in December 1732. Designed, so they said, for splendour and admiration, the theatre drew many new visitors to Covent Garden. Full every night, no doubt in part owing to the free tickets given to local harlots to entice men through its doors, the theatre became a known meeting place for those seeking pleasure and those offering it.

As for our house, situated conveniently near the theatre, most nights there was barely sufficient room to accommodate all our clients. Tom and I were glad of the additional business, despite working every waking hour and having precious few sleeping ones. We squeezed our way through the throngs in our establishment, smiling, serving, and exchanging a quip here and a confidence there, with the intent of making every customer feel at ease and ready with an open purse.

Henry Fielding, the novelist and satirist wrote about our premises in the prologue to his play *The Covent-Garden Tragedy,* a tale set in a brothel and first performed at the Theatre Royal, Drury Lane in June 1732. He included what became a well-known line, 'what rake is ignorant of King's Coffee-House?' 'None' was my heartfelt reply. It was my fervent hope that every rake in the city knew us well.

Shortly after the opening of the theatre Tom sired a second son by another woman. This child was christened Thomas at St. Paul's, Covent Garden on November 13, 1733. Gossips set their tongues wagging again, especially as I was at that time thirty-seven years of age and almost beyond birthing another child, but I paid no heed to what others said and Tom and I remained united. I had long ago decided that, in any circumstances, business came first. And ours prospered far too well to allow affairs of the heart, or the bedchamber, to interfere.

19. The first Covent Garden Theatre, plate 27 of *Microcosm of London*, 1808. The theatre burnt down the year this image was produced. Considered to be the golden age of British theatre it was a time of phenomenal expansion for the London theatre scene. Purpose-built candle-lit auditoriums hosted large numbers of people seeking to enjoy comedy, drama, music and other forms of entertainment.

Audiences were extremely lively and boisterous, generally consuming food and alcohol during the performances. The wealthier patrons occupied the boxes (so that they could both see and be seen) while the young men would eat and drink on benches at the front of the stalls. The pit was the place to find the prostitutes.

20. Detail from *The Rake's Rendez-Vous; or the Midnight Revels*, etching by George Bickham the Younger, *c.*1735, Trustees of the British Museum. A view inside Tom King's Coffee House with scenes of debauchery, a derivation from the tavern scene in Hogarth's *A Rake's Progress*. Little Tawny Betty can be seen behind the foreground table.

21. An 18th century bagnio scene, the Wellcome Collection, CC-BY 4.0.

CHAPTER 3

The Lure of Belsize House

By the latter years of the 1730s the proceeds of our various ventures in King's Coffee House were of such a magnitude that I was ready to further my ambitions.

Several other houses had set up in competition with us. Not all had good outcomes and none, not even those that did well, dented our profits or stole our custom. Those who came to King's knew full-well that they would not find greater delights, better service or more valuable sources of information in all of London and we were proud of our success.

Tom was happy enough to remain at King's. He had little ambition beyond comfort, company and a generous supply of grog, but my attention was by this time turned towards new pastures.

Many times over the years I had heard of Belsize House, centrepiece of the subordinate manor of Belsize, a large country house within the manor of Hampstead, some miles beyond the reaches of the city. Word reached me that this grand manor had become a house of pleasure – presenting those in my line of business with a wonderful opportunity. So I decided to seize upon the moment and offer my services there.

Belsize House lay just over four miles from the city and Covent Garden – a modest journey of less than one hour by horse or carriage. It would be a simple matter, I decided, to maintain our coffee-house while setting up a second business in the countryside. And in this manner I would make good my long-held plan to own a country residence.

Leaving Tom to oversee the business I travelled by carriage to view Belsize House for myself. At that time there were only a few scattered properties among the open green fields between Westminster, Tottenham Court and Belsize House. And what a splendid building it was, containing all-told 39 rooms, all of the utmost elegance and taste. Beyond the house lay an estate of some 234 acres of grounds, with walled gardens, fields and woods filled with deer for the hunt and a long and elegant tree-lined drive leading south west from Haverstock Hill.

The manor had been constructed seventy or more years previous, in the early 1660s, by Colonel Daniel O'Neill, a man of great wealth. Word has it that it was built as a gift for his wife, the Countess of Chesterfield. And if this were the truth, then what a gift to bestow; the manor was so well-provided that its forecourt could accommodate one hundred coaches.

By 1710 the manor house had been let to one Charles Povey who, having tried opening the gardens to the public, had abandoned the idea and, in 1720, leased the manor to another by the name of James Howell, a Welsh property speculator also known as 'the Welsh Ambassador'. He promptly opened the grounds to the public as pleasure gardens in which to ride or stroll while enjoying the beauty of the landscape and the fine country air. The house itself was also opened to the public, including the Great Room, beautifully decorated and large enough for balls, while throughout the manor visitors could admire exquisite and valuable paintings and furniture.

Soon Belsize Manor became a destination for the most well-to-do and aristocratic people in London. In 1721 it was graced by royalty, when the Prince of Wales (the future King George II) and Princess Caroline dined there. This of course, only served to enhance its popularity and thereafter visitors flocked to the house and grounds in ever greater numbers.

According to an edition of *The Daily Post* of 1720, the 'ancient and noble house' in Belsize had been made fit for entertainment during the summer season, with 'Dancing and Music', including illuminations in the gardens at night.

22. Belsize House illustration, *c*.1721, later hand colour, promoting the house, the park, the wilderness and gardens all 'wonderfully improved'.

The Daily Post.

TUESDAY, MAY 12, 1720.

Leyden, May 9.

We hear that the Earl of Marchmont, one of the sixteen Peers for North Britain, is soon to be marry'd to the Countess Dowager of Eglintoun.

Since the Overturning of his Majesty's Coach last Saturday Night, some more Hobby Grooms are to be appointed to carry Lanthorns or Moons before their Majesties Coaches in the Night-time.

The Chapel of Lincoln's Inn, which has been shut for some Time, in order to repair and beautify the same, was open'd on Sunday last, and is now very handsome, there being a new Pulpit, a new Desk for the Chaplain, and another for the Clerk, adorn'd with Purple Velvet and Gold Trimming; but the fine painted Glass to the Windows is not yet finish'd; so that only Part is at yet put up.

23. An example of *The Daily Post* masthead dated May 12, 1720.

24. *Brothel Scene*, detail, Nicolaus Knüpfer, 1650, Rijksmuseum Amsterdam – the historic costumes suggest the painting was based on a play. The visit to Belsize House and gardens by the Prince and Princess of Wales in 1721 prompted large numbers of visitors wishing to sample the delights on offer. But within a year, the disgraceful gambling, folly and voraciousness got completely out of hand in the 'house of pleasure' and vice trumped virtue at Belsize House.

25. Previously known as New Spring Gardens – *The Grand Walk, Vauxhall Gardens,* Canaletto, *c.*1751. London's pleasure gardens of the period were places where wealthy members of society as well as leaders and followers of high fashion socialised. The gardens were also popular with the middle classes, possibly expecting to be entertained by the unseemly behaviour and debauchery that abounded. Admission to Vauxhall Gardens was only a shilling and for most people, affordable. Entertainments of all kinds were provided and the gardens boasted broad, promenading avenues, narrow pathways, wooded groves and plenty of secluded 'dark walks' for lovers. And if seeking a discreet assignation a visitor might well encounter a well-dressed prostitute.
According to William Howitt in *The Northern Heights of London,* although smaller in scale than those of Vauxhall and Ranelagh, 'none of the above places could exceed [the gardens of] Belsize House'.

'Visitors could fish or hunt in the grounds, dine on the best food, enjoy the finest wines, and dance in the spectacular ballroom,' the paper informed its readers. As the 1720s progressed the manor became one of the most popular places to see and be seen. James Howell announced in 1725 that

> Belsize House is open every day; the public days are Mondays, Thursdays and Saturdays, with a good concert of music in the Long Gallery during the whole season.

However there was more afoot than the simple pleasures of fresh air and wholesome pursuits. Author Daniel Defoe, the very same one that I was reputed to have encountered in Newgate Gaol, reported that Howell had made the mansion into 'a true house of pleasure.' 'In the Gardens and in the House,' he wrote, 'Howell entertained with all kinds of Game... This attracted many people to the Place, for they were so effectively ratified in all sorts of diversions, that the Wicked part at length broke in.'

What, I wonder, can he mean? Well, it seems that James Howell's plan had been to entice to Belsize House not only the cream of the nobility but the cream of London's courtesans also, and with their arrival the delights of the place were soon to include licentious and ribald goings-on, alongside the concerts and the family entertainment. One wag recorded that 'The scandalous, lewd house that's call'd Belsize, where sharpers lurk, yet vice in public lies, is publicly become a rendezvous of strumpets...'

This made the lure of the house even more enticing and by the mid 1730s Belsize House was known to be the most pleasurable of all the pleasure gardens around London, outdoing even the famed New Spring Gardens, re-opened as Vauxhall Gardens in Kennington, south of the city. Indeed the large number of carriages of visiting nobility and gentry caused frequent jams on the wide driveway leading to the house from Haverstock Hill.

Learning of all this and seeing the great house for myself after travelling there, I spied a perfect opportunity – both for business and for my remove to the countryside. If I were to find a house of my own in the area and bring the best of my girls to reside in it, they could hasten to Belsize House daily to parade and entice and offer delights of the flesh to such gentlemen as went there seeking those gratifications.

26. Well Walk Hampstead and the original well in 1911, from an original by A. R. Quinton.
In 1814, John James Park recalled in *The Topography and Natural History of Hampstead,* 'Although the Well Walk and its surroundings were at this period frequented by a good and even fashionable class, it relied to a great extent upon the patronage of the pleasure-hunting multitude of London.' Consequently the good people 'gradually withdrew themselves from the scene leaving it ultimately to the rakish and disreputable element... We have Court Ladies that are all Air and no Dress; City Ladies, that are over-dress'd and no Air'... and 'Country Dames... their Cloathes hang as loose about 'em as their Reputations.'

Park also noted that the Hampstead Wells had deteriorated under the influence of Mother Huff's establishment. And that 'indeed it appears that Hampstead came in for its full share of folly and indecorum.' Furthermore, 'the general dissoluteness of the period under consideration must be a matter of lamentation and disgust to every refined mind.' Daniel Defoe wrote in 1724, 'As there is (especially at the Wells) a conflux of all sorts of company, even Hampstead itself has suffered in its good name and you see sometimes more gallantry than modesty.'

27. *The Beggar's Opera* dramatist John Gay (1685-1732), National Galleries of Scotland. John Park said, 'the loss of his fortune... had affected Gay so nearly, as almost to prove fatal to him. After suffering some time under a violent cholic, he removed to Hampstead in 1729 for the benefit of the air and waters, where, by the care of his friends, among whom Arbuthnot and Pope appear to have shown particular tenderness, his health was restored.'

When I returned to Covent Garden I was eager to put my plans into motion as soon as possible. Tom bid me go ahead, he had not the energy or the desire to accompany me. He was beginning to suffer with the ill-effects of his years of drinking and I pointed out to him that an occasional remove to some country air would do him good, but he showed no enthusiasm, while I knew that without doubt this was an opportunity not to be missed.

I soon realised that in addition to Belsize House there was much to be enjoyed. Aside from the delights of the country air and scenery, a carriage ride up the hill beyond Belsize to Hampstead High Street enabled visitors to sample the beneficial pleasures of the Hampstead Wells and its spa waters. I learnt that these chalybeate, or mineral spring waters were impregnated with salts of iron and in much demand, as were those of the Royal Bagnigge Wells which was situated just a few miles away and was once the summer residence of the famed Nell Gwynne, actress and mistress to King Charles II.

As I made my plans I knew that I wasn't going to be the only Moll in the Hampstead and Belsize area. Mother Huff's place had been established on the Spaniards Road – once the haunt of highwaymen – between *Jack Straw's Castle* and *The Spaniards* tollgate inn since 1678. She had later moved to *The Hoop and Bunch of Grapes* at North End, Hampstead in 1728. Her tavern was licensed to sell alcohol, while tea could be taken in the gay gardens and cakes, cheesecakes and the best entertainment were to be had. The notorious Mother Huff was particularly adept at assisting her visitors in their assignations. But she was by this time aged and I was confident that mine would be an establishment more than equal to hers.

Coincidentally, or not, I would also be associated with a man called Hoff. But I am getting ahead of myself. Let me explain how I set up my business on Haverstock Hill.

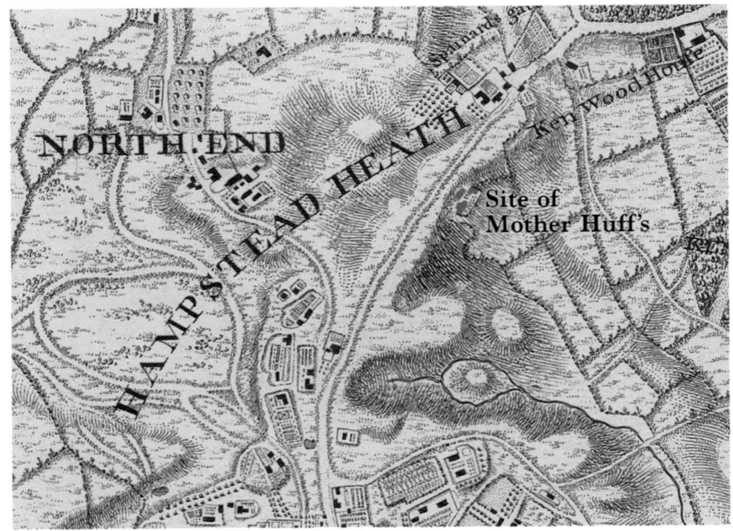

28. Part of John Rocque's 1746 map with the site of Mother Huff's tavern and tea gardens on Spaniards Road marked in red. John Rocque's sixteen-sheet map of London and its environs was entitled: *An Exact Survey of London, Westminster and Southwark, and the Country near Ten Miles Round, begun in 1741 and ended in 1745.*

29. *The Fleet River near Bagnigge Wells*, (anonymous). A few smaller pleasure gardens were also open to visitors. Since 1680, there was Bagnigge House, located near *The Pindar of Wakefield* by the River Fleet in Clerkenwell and fed from a spring on Hampstead Heath. Bagnigge Wells House was originally Nell Gwynne's summer residence. Eleanor (Nell) Gwyn (1650-1687) was an actress and long time mistress of King Charles II. Bagnigge had become a place of entertainment for Londoners, acquiring its reputation following the discovery of two mineral springs in the garden.

30. Bagnigge Wells once stood between King's Cross Road and Pakenham Street, engraving by William Henry Prior, 1780, later hand colour. Originally produced for *Old and New London*.

31. *A Bagnigge Wells Scene, or No Resisting Temptation*, published by Carrington Bowles, Trustees of the British Museum. This scene features two park walkers. One young woman is plucking a rose from a flowerbed while another looks on, raising her dress to reveal her petticoat beneath.

32. *A View of Hampstead Road near Tom King's House,* J. B. Chatelain, 1750, later hand colour, British Museum. A short portion of the single track Hampstead Road (lower left, now renamed Haverstock Hill) with an isolated house at far left. The view is over fields, with only one other visible dwelling standing between these houses and the City of London in the distance.

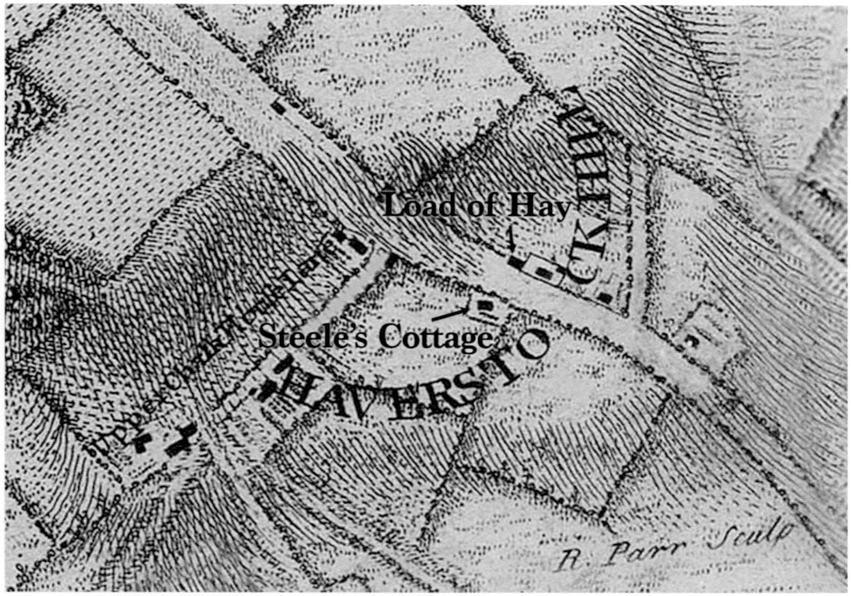

33. Portion of John Rocque's map of the Haverstock Hill area in 1746 with the original *Load of Hay* tavern and Richard Steele's Cottage marked. Local residents used to travel along the road to and from town on horseback.

CHAPTER 4

Move to the Country

One evening a couple of wealthy land-owning customers at the coffee-house told me of an opportunity to acquire a parcel of land on the road to Hampstead, just by a tavern named *The Load of Hay*. I determined to go and view the land for myself, taking a carriage out of the city the following day. And I was well pleased with what I found. *The Load of Hay* appeared to be a convivial establishment and the land beside it was ideal for my intentions. I could measure the distance from London exactly as there was a four-mile stone just outside the tavern. A good distance – close enough to the city to be able to travel back and forth with relative ease, but far enough to be able to offer the fresh air and green delights of the countryside.

It so happened that Tom knew of this area; the land just across the Hampstead Road, adjacent to the plots we wished to purchase, belonged to his *alma mater*, Eton College and was named the Chalcots.

The location, I could see immediately, was ideal. *The Load of Hay,* which previously bore the name *The Cart and Horses,* had been opened in 1721 and it had become an important staging post for travellers venturing to Hampstead from London. A picturesque inn with a lovely tea garden, it was used for the exchange of coach horses. Stables behind the inn were kept for horses brought in for travellers to use in addition to their own horses to assist with the journey up the steep hill that lay beyond.

Having our property in such close proximity would allow us, and our guests, to take advantage of the availability of additional horses, should they be required. But most importantly, the tavern attracted many travellers – those with carriages, with wagons and with carts, journeying both in and out of London. Perfect for my intended venture. And I knew that, should Howell's enterprise fail and there be no business for us at the manor house, there would still be plenty of trade thanks to *The Load of Hay*.

The purchase was concluded without delay and I was able to put the next part of my plan into effect – the building of several adjoining residences. The first we built for ourselves and it was described by others as a 'very genteel country house'. Next to this we built a property to accommodate the working girls I intended to bring with me. This we called the second or middle house. A further property was later added, but for the time being these two sufficed very well. In addition to these two houses we acquired the use of a property very close to Belsize House. This enabled the girls to hasten there with their culls, as desires overcame them, in order to fulfil their requirements with as little inconvenience as possible. The satisfied customers having departed, the girls then refreshed their garments and coiffure before returning to the Manor to parade in the gardens, catching the eye of others requiring our services.

I had not long removed to my new house when, looking out of the window I spied some young gentlemen riding out towards Hampstead, no doubt for the air. As they drew level with my home one of them proclaimed loudly 'Look yonder, there's Moll King's Folly!' I smiled, wondering what constituted this 'folly'? Were they remarking upon the nature of my business or the design of my house? Or did they term 'folly' my move out of Covent Garden to Belsize?

I leaned forward through the window and addressed them, remarking, 'No, it's your Folly, and that of some others as silly as yourself, and they help'd to build it for me.' At which they, taking in good part my comment, roared with merrie laughter and continued on their way.

Perhaps my house attracted these young men's notice because it was a timber-framed building. As most new constructions at that time were of stone, this 'Tudor' style, having its origins two centuries before, was considered by most to be very dated. I paid no heed to that; the house was just as I wished it to be and I found it charming.

34. *View from 'Moll Kings House' in 1760* with harvesting scene, later hand colour, by William Henry Prior from *Old and New London*. This engraving was made ten years after *A View of Hampstead Road near Tom King's House* seen in figure 32. Apart from the harvesting activities the main difference to the scene is that the house on the left is far more detailed, revealing that it was gabled.

35. *Richard Steele's Cottage*, published *c.*1880, later hand colour. The cottage stood just across Haverstock Hill from Moll King's house. It was pulled down in 1867. The site of the house and its garden is now marked by a row of houses called Steele's Terrace and the *Sir Richard Steele* pub. Writing from this cottage to Pope on June 1, 1712, Steele said, 'I am at a solitude, an house between Hampstead and London, where in Sir Charles Sedley died.'

36. Close view of part of the Kings' original timber-framed gabled property from the 1760 engraving as seen in figure 34.

37. Sir Richard Steele is recorded as using the Haverstock Hill cottage in the early 1700s. John Park, in his *Topography of Hampstead* noted that 'in the same house in which Sir Charles Sedley died, afterwards resided a wit [Richard Steele] who resembled him too nearly in the licentiousness of his manners, though he rose far superior to him in the integrity of his heart.'

Ours was not the only dwelling constructed of wood. The tavern next door was also timber-framed, as was the cottage across the way, which had previously been occupied by Sir Richard Steele, an Irish writer, playwright and politician who with his friend Joseph Addison had founded a well-respected little publication by the name of *The Spectator.*

It was said that he moved to the modest dwelling opposite mine to escape the duns (debt collectors) who were hard on his tail for gambling debts. It seems he was not a lucky man at the card tables. Or elsewhere – I heard tell that along with six others, he had once entered into an alchemical experiment to make gold. Another gamble that failed and as a consequence he was the butt of many a comic jibe.

In his writing Sir Richard professed high moral virtues which, like so many of his ilk, it seemed he was unable to apply to his own conduct. Gossips had it that he fathered an illegitimate child, Elizabeth, by the daughter of the founder of the Kit-Kat Club, of which Steele was a member. The Kit-Kat Club was established for the furtherance of the Whig objectives and it took its name from the mutton pies, known as Kit Cats and named after the innkeeper, Christopher Catt, whose establishment was the venue for the club's first meetings.

Club members met during the summer months at *The Upper Flask* tavern at the top of the hill in Hampstead. Sir Richard was collected from his cottage by Arbuthnot, Pope and other members and taken from there by coach to the weekly meetings.

It seems that the coach was usually more necessary at the end than at the beginning of the evening, for the man of many moral precepts against drinking was better at preaching than at practice – all the while protesting to his beloved wife back in London that he was too tired to make the journey home. Not the first gentleman to make such protestations.

Sir Richard was clearly quite a fellow and I was sorry I had not known him, as he departed this life in 1729. He was, apparently, sympathetic to prostitutes and had stated as much in *The Spectator.*

During the time my far larger house was under construction I had amused myself by imagining the goings-on in his charming cottage as Steele played host to his friends from the Kit-Kat Club.

38. *The Upper Flask* tavern sold flasks of water from the Hampstead Spa in the 18th century. The Kit-Kat Club held their summer meetings in a private room there. Virtually opposite the tavern the shallow Whitestone Pond was intended for the benefit of tired horses after hauling carts and carriages up the hill.

39. The Duke of Kingston presenting his daughter Mary Pierrepont to members of the Kit-Kat Club. The custom of toasting ladies after dinner was peculiar to the club, and was described as The Knights of the 'Toast'.

In the *Tatler* No. 24 Joseph Addison wrote, 'Though this institution had so trivial a beginning, it is now elevated into a formal order, and that happy virgin, who is received and drunk to at their meetings, has no more to do in this life but to judge and accept of the first good offer.' In *The Annals of Hampstead* Thomas Barratt declared that the young girl 'went from the lap of one poet, or patriot, or statesman to the arms of another, feasted with sweetmeats, or overwhelmed with caresses...' Today this behaviour would be seen very differently indeed.

My home was built speedily thanks to my close connections with some of the best builders and carpenters from Soho and Covent Garden. And once it was completed I wasted no time in gathering together some of the finest young harlots, dressing them well and sending them out to parade their wares in the gardens of Belsize House.

I was able to add to their number by offering help to young girls travelling to London on the coaches that stopped at *The Load of Hay*. Coaching stations were known to be the place to find innocent young country girls coming to the city. I followed Mother Needham's practice, making sure they had a bed for the night and food, reassuring them all the while that they were safe and would find work in the area. Once procured in this way they had little option but to accept my protection and join my 'stable of girls' and when I had set them to work I ensured that they repaid my generosity in full.

While settled in Belsize, I travelled regularly to Covent Garden to see what my pretty birds (customers) were doing. Tom, with Black Betty by his side to assist, had taken charge of the coffee-house. But his health was declining rapidly, he had taken far too many tankards of ale, the alcohol had addled his brain and sickened his body and in 1737, to my great sadness, he died. We buried him on October 11 in St. Paul's churchyard in Covent Garden. Tom had been my companion for over twenty years.

While I, along with our son Charles, missed his company, I had been no fool when it came to our property. I made sure that our land in Belsize and our properties there were all in my name. Tom had ownership of the various goods and chattels relating to King's Coffee House, the Hart Street room and two other houses in Hampstead. Careful reading of my husband's will provided no clues as to where these two houses were located. There was no information regarding the name under which they were listed, nor the purpose to which the houses were put, although any who knew my line of business might guess.

40. Cottage used as a brothel outside London, Illustration by Robert Cruikshank from *The English Spy,* Charles Molloy Westmacott, 1825-26. This picture from the later Regency period shows that the principles of the 'working cottage' were the same as in Mary King's day.

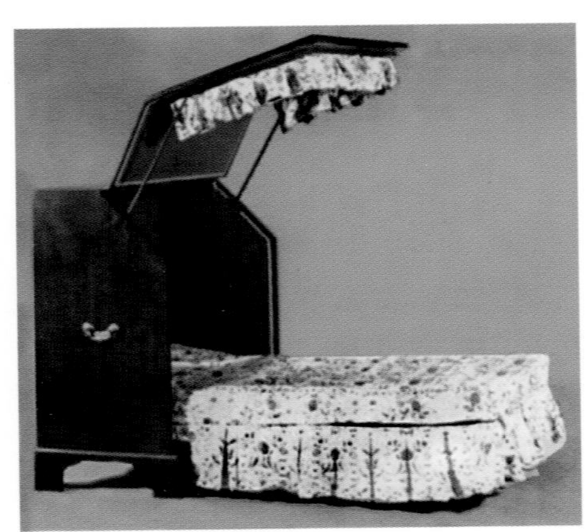

41. Bureau bedstead, Christies, New York. Oliver Goldsmith in 1769 described such an item of dual-purpose furniture:

> The whitewashed wall, the nicely sanded floor,
> The varnished clock that clicked behind the door,
> The chest contrived a double debt to pay,
> A bed at night, a chest of drawers by day.

This veil of obscurity was intentional on our part. I was determined that those searching for evidence of my profession would find virtually no entries in the Court Rolls that might throw light on these matters.

Tom's will is another matter. The preponderance of turn-up bedsteads in almost every room in our houses might have given an observant outsider reason to pause and wonder. Many people found these bedsteads, disguised as other items of furniture, quite charming, and they became the height of fashion. And they certainly suited our requirements, enabling our houses to appear as other homes, disguising their true purpose.

Thankfully none did appear concerned and when I was granted administration of his estate all the items he owned reverted to me. The inventory of Tom's possessions included a walnut or wainscot turn-up bedstead in each bedroom of the two upper floors of one house, each with a feather bed, bolster and pillows. In addition there were mahogany chests, scarlet China window curtains, window seats, six mahogany chairs with leather seats, a walnut dining table, plus easy chairs. There was a lovely walnut eight-day clock on the staircase and the downstairs front parlour had a wainscot turn-up bedstead and a mahogany dining table plus six chairs, an easy chair and cushions. We even had a bedstead in the nicely-appointed back parlour.

All these items, and those just as fine in our other houses, had been purchased with money we had earned through our many years as proprietors of King's Coffee House. I delighted in owning such furniture. How far I had come since my start in life, in that gloomy garret in Vine Street.

42. Covent Garden Strawberry seller.

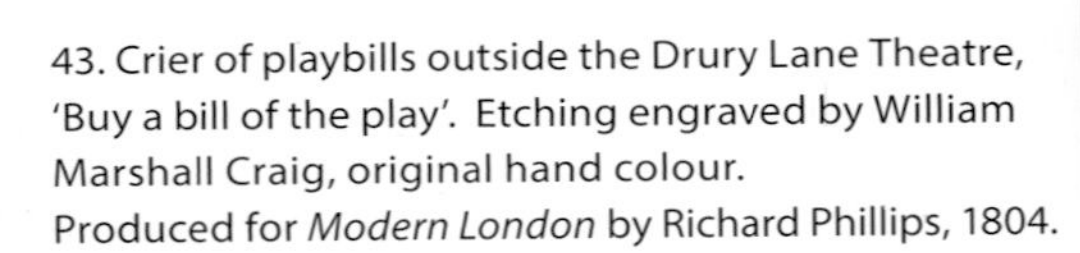

43. Crier of playbills outside the Drury Lane Theatre, 'Buy a bill of the play'. Etching engraved by William Marshall Craig, original hand colour.
Produced for *Modern London* by Richard Phillips, 1804.

44. *Bachelors Fare or Bread and Cheese with Kisses*, detail, after John Collett, *c*.1778, published by Carrington Bowles of St. Paul's Churchyard.
The scene at first seems innocent enough but the client is actually giving the young woman coins in return for her sexual favours.

CHAPTER 5

A Dish with Moll

After Tom's passing I continued to run the Covent Garden coffee-house, while also overseeing my business in Belsize. I went regularly between the two, relying only on those few whom I knew I could trust and watching everyone like a mother hawk. Many now referred to our place as Moll King's, a compliment I took as my due since the business had, in truth, always been more mine than Tom's. From the start I had taken charge of the supplies and the staff, while also keeping the accounting books. However I had Tom's name – and presence – to shield me and now that he was gone, as a woman with full charge of a business, I encountered plenty of difficulties – those who would not have dealings with me, those who told me I had no place giving orders, and those who would rob me, thinking me a fool. I gave short shrift to all. And I was rightly proud that King's – Moll King's – continued to be as popular as ever, with those of all classes visiting to sup ale, coffee or chocolate, to pleasure themselves with my girls and to enjoy the gossip of the day. It was said that my coffee-house was a place where 'the rules of polite conduct were temporarily suspended' and that gratified me, for it was just as I intended.

After the evening's performances were over, the actress-harlots from the nearby theatres, known as the Toasts of the Town, would arrive at King's dressed in their finery to have what they termed 'a dish with Moll'. Alongside the actresses, marketers and dandies would sit lords of the highest rank, many of whom came with their ladies.

45. *Morning*, from *The Four Times of Day* series, William Hogarth, 1736. Outside the entrance to King's Coffee House, which is repositioned in front of St. Paul's Church. Early on a winter's morning a woman stands aghast at the sight of revellers and a pair of dishevelled rakes fondling some of the girls. In his *Club Life of London,* John Timbs recalled 'Noblemen and the first beaux, after leaving Court, would go to the house in full dress, with swords and bags, and in rich brocaded silk coats, and walked and conversed with persons of every description.'

He also noted that 'A concourse of arts, literary characters and other men of genius frequented the numerous coffee-houses, wine and cider-cellars, etc., within the boundaries of Covent Garden. Butler, Addison, Sir R. Steele, Otway, Dryden, Pope, Warburton, Cibber, Fielding, Churchill, Bolingbroke, and Dr. Johnson; Rich, Woodward, Booth, Wilkes, Garrick, and Macklin; Kitty Clive, "Peg" Woffington, Mrs. Pritchard, the Duchess of Bolton, Lady Derby, Lady Thurlow, and the Duchess of St. Alban's; Sir Peter Lely, Sir Godfrey Kneller, and Sir James Thornhill; Vandevelde, Zincke, Lambert, Hogarth, Hayman, Wilson, Dance, Meyer, and Samuel Foote. But even to this list it would be possible to make many additions.'

Then there were the scholars, philosophers and writers, among them Henry Fielding, John Gay and Alexander Pope, all of whom were frequent patrons.

Among my regulars was William Hogarth – the very same who had painted Mother Needham. He featured our establishment in his picture *Morning,* one of a set of four paintings titled *Morning, Noon, Evening* and *Night,* in 1736. The engravings of this set were published in 1738 and later on Hogarth painted my portrait, although sadly it was a less flattering image than I might have wished for. Still, no matter, with that picture came greater notoriety for me and for King's and we continued to attract the most illustrious of clientele.

There were those – reformers and religious types – who opposed me at every turn, expressing disgust at our activities, badmouthing me and attempting to have us closed down, but they did not succeed. Although I did get into quite a few quarrels over the years which cost me handsome sums of money. Upwards of twenty indictments were preferred against me at the Grand Jury at Westminster Hall for keeping a disorderly house. But as my accusers failed to find any evidence that I was running a bawdy-house I always managed to extricate myself from any charges at minimal expense. One of my most persistent detractors was Justice of the Peace John Gonson. He was determined to close down bagnios and brothels by conducting raids and he sent his spies to King's, hoping to find evidence he could use to shut us down. He was a nuisance, but I was able to outwit him with a private coded language I had contrived with my most trusted employees and others, an excellent device for befuddling the likes of the magistrate, who eventually ceased to trouble us.

Our critics were few, most enjoyed our hospitality and whatever delights King's had to offer. In fact our fame only increased and on one memorable eve we had the honour of a visit from none other than the king himself – King George II, accompanied by his equerry Viscount Gage. Unfortunately the king had to cut short his visit, having been challenged to a fight for admiring the companion of one of his neighbours. After he departed I was aglow with pride; if only Tom had been there to see royalty step through our door.

As King's continued to be the perfect haunt for nobles and men of letters, rakes and prostitutes of every type and my fortunes prospered, I could, and did, lend money to many of my most favoured customers – naturally on the basis that they would repay it promptly with a generous amount of interest.

And as with my country enterprise, I was also ready to offer financial assistance and the benefit of my advice to any girl who needed to set herself up as a courtesan.

The official mourning period for a widow was a year, and out of respect for Tom's memory I waited that long before taking matrimonial vows once again, this time with John Hoff, a skilled carpenter of St. Anne's, Westminster. I had known him for some while by then as he had charge of the construction of my half-timbered house in Haverstock Hill. I found him pleasing enough and so we were married on October 11, 1738 at St. Dunstan-in-the-West, the guild church for the Worshipful Company of Cordwainers (shoemakers), situated in Fleet Street. St. Dunstan was the patron saint of goldsmiths and, fittingly, the church wardens included members of the Hoare banking family, whose bank had stood opposite the church since 1690. All of which sat well with me, since I came from a family of shoemakers and I was particularly fond of making money.

Gossips had claimed that John was marrying me for my money, but if that were true he had no opportunity to lay his hands on it. Just over three months after our marriage we received yet another indictment for running a disorderly house. It was served to 'John Hoffe of the parish of Saint Paul Covent Garden within the Liberty of Westminster in the County of Middlesex, Yeoman and Mary his Wife' on January 23, 1739. And within fifteen days of that upset, he sadly departed this life on February 6, having appointed me as his executrix and leaving all his worldly goods to me.

His will was proved on February 9, and I buried him in St. Paul's churchyard Covent Garden, on February 14, the day of the feast of St. Valentine. Notwithstanding any speculation on the somewhat hasty departure of John Hoff, having buried two husbands within 16 months, all the while carrying the full burden of running the coffee-house and the business on Haverstock Hill, I must confess I did begin to drink rather heavily while keeping company with my clients.

Where once I would not touch a drop in order to keep my attention sharp, I now found liquor a comfort as my bones began to ache and my responsibilities to feel heavy.

46. Etching with engraving, later hand colour, featuring the finery of the clothing in a drawing room at the Court of St. James's, mid 18th century, Yale University, Lewis Walpole Library. Part of the monarch's canopied throne is visible in the background.

47. *He and his Drunken Companions raise a Riot in Covent Garden,* anonymous, etching *c.*1735.
A version of a scene on the piazza depicting drunken rakes and friends accosting every passing woman. Armed with staves, the watch attempt to suppress the riot.

Working girls were generally blamed for local disturbances and the occasional riot. But actually it was the young drunken rakes who generally caused most of the trouble. Gin, widely available, was responsible for most of the drunkenness in London.

I employed men dressed as footmen to protect our girls and keep my customers' drunken behaviour under control. But, perhaps inevitably after drinking all night, revellers in high spirits would spill out onto the pavement (an image Mr. Hogarth depicted in one of his works) which resulted in more charges against me. One night a truly riotous affray erupted inside the Long Room with drunkards brawling out in the piazza and as a result I was charged, given fines and a term of three months in Newgate Gaol. I was in Newgate from June to September of 1739 and as by then I was no youngster, being 43 years of age, the foul conditions in the prison took a toll on my health.

During my imprisonment my nephew had overseen the coffee-house and after I was released I decided to leave him in charge in Covent Garden and to spend most of my time in my place on Haverstock Hill. Here the country air and quieter neighbourhood pleased me and I was less inclined to visit the city.

My business in Belsize was still doing well, with my girls housed next door and using the rented property close to Belsize House to service their customers. However, the heyday of that mansion and its grounds was drawing to a close. James Howell's visitors had increased to such an extent that, not unsurprisingly, public outrage grew over what were considered by many to be unacceptable activities. The local magistrates had been instructed to act against the 'deteriorating, unseemly and riotous behaviour' taking place under Howell's reign, but it was not until 1745 that Belsize House was finally closed.

It was the end of an era. We had enjoyed great success and I was financially comfortable, so it was without regret that I let my girls go on their way, thanking them for serving me well, and retired to the charming villa I had built behind my house.

18th century fashion print.

Moll King's Legacy

48. St. Paul's Covent Garden today.

Extract from the *London Evening Post* for September 1747:

Last Wednesday died, at her house at Hampstead, after a long illness, Mrs. King, who for many years kept a noted Night House in Covent Garden Market, known by the name of Moll King's Coffee House.

Extract from *Covent Garden in Mourning,* 1747:

No Drams will now the Constables invite,
The Spir'tuous Bribe upon a Frosty Night:
Sunk are their Fees, their Usuals are no more,
And Moll is gone, the Glims infernal roar:
Thro' the Piazza hollow Winds return,
That Moll is gone, and all the Watchmen mourn.
O! wast it round ye Watchmen, as ye cry
The Hours of Night, and Moll is gone reply.

Anon, printed and published by B. Dickinson, Leadenhall Street

CHAPTER 6

Moll King and Nancy Dawson

Mary King would outlive John Hoff by eight years – she died at her Haverstock Hill home on September 17, 1747, two years after Belsize House closed its doors for good. She was buried as Mary Hoff, recorded as 'Widow, from Hampstead in Middlesex' on September 27 in the churchyard of St. Paul's, Covent Garden, ending her tumultuous life as she would have wished, back in her old hunting ground and in the same graveyard as both her husbands.

John Hoff had left all his worldly goods to Mary and she left everything she had in trust to her only son Charles, then nineteen, to be administered by two executors, one of them from St. Martin-in-the-Fields. Charles inherited the whole of his mother's estate in 1758 when he turned 30.

Mary thoroughly understood the property business. She knew for example the difference between tenants-in-common and joint tenancy. She stated in her will that all copyholds and personal estates the children of her son Charles should inherit should do so as tenants-in-common. If Charles did not have any children then everything was to go to the Rector, churchwardens, overseers or trustees of the Parish of St. Giles-in-the-Fields, but only to be used for the benefit of the poor children of the parish, where Mary herself had once lived.

Whether Mary's will meant that Charles was indeed the only son born of her loins, or whether she meant her only surviving son, is not clear – until one learns more about her husband Tom King's second son, young Tom King.

49. *Nancy Dawson*, copy by Samuel de Wilde after an anonymous mezzotint, the Garrick Club Collection. The original artist of this design might have been Edward Penny (1714-1791). Nancy is shown dancing her celebrated hornpipe. In this portrait she wears green shoes with paste buckles, a round yellow straw hat edged with blue ribbon, and a short white dress open at the front to reveal a pink underskirt over which she has a spotted muslin apron. According to the Garrick club records 'Contemporary memoirs accounted her a woman of great beauty and grace, with a shrewish temper, who led a notoriously immoral life.'

50. Staymaker at work in the 18th century.

Young Tom, as we know, was born in 1733, but there is no listing in the *Record of Old Westminsters* of his attendance at this school or any other which fits with this time period. There is however a record of a Thomas King's burial at St. Paul's Covent Garden on October 29, 1734 when Tom would have been about a year old. This is about the time that Tom senior's health began to decline and one can only wonder if little Tom's birth and early death led to his father's decline. The death rate in London during the 1700s was particularly high and it was not uncommon for up to one in five young children to die before their second birthday.

Although his baptism record states that Thomas senior and his wife Mary registered the baptism, it appears from the available information that both of them were begetting children by other partners. First came Charles, son of Mary and an unknown man; then came little Tom, fathered by Tom and an unknown woman. So while Mary accepted Tom into the family, he was almost certainly not her son and the records relating to Mary's life support this hypothesis.

After Moll's death we do not know what happened to the timber-framed house and the middle house. But there is general agreement that at some point, famed dancer and actress Nancy Dawson moved into the small villa set behind them. How did that come about? There had to be a significant connection between the Kings' estate and Nancy. What was it?

Nancy Dawson was the stage name of a woman who, research indicates, was baptised Ann Newton in Axminster, Devon, on January 17, 1728. This is substantiated by her will, in which she named her father as William Newton of Martlett Court, Covent Garden. He was a staymaker – a craft practised mainly by men, as making corsets through the manipulation of whalebone and the stitching through of layers of stiffened cloth demanded especially strong hands. This was a very well-paid, skilled trade with a plentiful clientele since the fashion of the times demanded that middle and upper class women wear stays. And around Covent Garden there were two professions which had particular need of corset makers such as William Newton – prostitution and the theatre.

Ann Newton was associated with both.

51. Scene from John Gay's *The Beggar's Opera* VI, Act 3, Scene 2, William Hogarth. This version, now in the Tate Gallery, was painted in 1731 (*The Beggar's Opera was* first performed in 1728).

52. Nancy Dawson portrait, James Watson, *c.*1762, New York Public Library.

Apparently Mary King's 'pupil' (although in precisely which disciplines is not stated) either by inference or association, was considered a loose woman. Although to be fair, that was the consensus opinion of all women who were in the theatre. In discussing her association with the Haverstock Hill property I'll use Ann's stage name, Nancy.

In 1744, then aged sixteen, Nancy Dawson was taught to dance by the puppet master Griffin. At that time Mary King was mostly based in Hampstead. Some accounts have Nancy working in the taverns for a number of years and probably also in Moll King's Coffee House, well *before* she went to the Drury Lane Theatre as a dancer. There, in 1756, her seven-year theatre career began in earnest. Nancy was to become an overnight success three years later at the age of 31, when she stood in for the leading comic dancer of the hornpipe, in the 1759 Drury Lane revival of John Gay's ballad opera in three acts, *The Beggar's Opera.* It was generally agreed that the salaciousness of her dancing contributed greatly to her reputation. Contemporary memoirs accounted her 'a woman of great beauty and grace, but with a shrewish temper, heartless and mercenary who led a notoriously immoral life.' However, modern authors Olive Baldwin and Thelma Wilson, looking into the life of Nancy Dawson, consider this reputation undeserved. They write:

> The tune to which she danced her hornpipe quickly became popular and many ballads were set to it, prints of her were published, and her image appeared on snuff boxes and tiles. Like other eighteenth-century female theatre performers, she was slandered in a so-called *Genuine Memoir*. The name 'Nancy Dawson' was used for race horses and ships, and after her death in 1767 the tune 'Nancy Dawson' took on a life of its own. By the mid-nineteenth century, the tune's popularity with sailors, and a set of bawdy words made to it, led to the belief that Nancy herself had been nothing more than a prostitute, but a close look at what can be discovered about her career and her personal life gives a rather different picture.

Written by the theatrical composer Dr. Thomas A. Arne, today we know the hornpipe melody as that of the nursery rhyme *Here We Go Round the Mulberry Bush*. But the words of two verses out of the eight-verse song titled

The Ballad of Nancy Dawson, and attributed to George Alexander Stevens, were certainly different from that of the children's rhyme:

> Of all the girls in our town,
> The black, the fair, the red, the brown,
> That dance and prance it up and down,
> There's none like Nancy Dawson.
>
> Her easy mien, her shape so neat,
> She foots, she trips, she looks so sweet,
> Her ev'ry motion is complete.
> I die for Nancy Dawson.

And an alternative couple of verses from the New York Public Library digital collections:

> How easily she trips the stage,
> Her heaving breasts all eyes engage,
> Loves fire she can best assuage,
> O charming Nancy Dawson.
>
> Yet vainly each breast alarms,
> With all love's hoard of heavenly charms,
> She's only for N–d S––rs arms,
> The smiling Nancy Dawson.

Thomas Barratt recorded in *The Annals of Hampstead,*

> Nancy Dawson, the famous hornpipe-dancer, who gained fame and fortune by her nimble exploits in *The Beggar's Opera,* ended her days in a snug retreat on Haverstock Hill ... some 20 years after she had captivated the town by her dancing. The song which celebrated her beauty remained in vogue – because of its catching air – to a much later date.

Interestingly, Thomas Barratt's account does not connect that snug retreat with the Mary King-Hoff estate, and he would have Nancy starting her dancing career in 1747 which is aged 19, some three years after she had met Griffin; 12 years prior to her hornpipe triumph and the year that Mary King died.

It is on record that Nancy retired prematurely from the stage in 1763, thereafter residing in the Haverstock Hill villa. Here she died just under four years later on June 9, 1767, the date confirmed in the *Biographical Dictionary of Actors and Actresses etc. 1660-1800.* Nancy was buried on June 12, in the joint cemetery of St George's Holborn and St. George's, Bloomsbury next to the Foundling Hospital. Nancy requested that she be buried in a grey coffin with white nails and plumes.

A large gravestone was installed, but its original inscription which read 'Here lies Nancy Dawson', with presumably some dates and other details, is now indecipherable. According to the *Biographical Dictionary of Actors and Actresses* (as well as several nineteenth-century sources) 'the inscription on her headstone supposedly consisted of eight lines of a disreputable ditty commencing "Nancy Dawson was a whore" and a rector had the stone turned down flat, with the inscription underneath, so as not to offend those who used the grounds for pleasant walks.'

53. The spire of St. George's, Bloomsbury. The church was built by Nicholas Hawksmoor, protégé of Sir Christopher Wren, topped with a statue of George I dressed in a Roman toga, it is considered the most eccentric spire in London.

Nancy Dawson left the theatre suddenly. One season she was on the December 1763 programme bill and the next, she wasn't. For such a celebrated dancer to have departed the scene of her triumphs without a mention is highly unusual. One can only surmise that she had found herself in the family way, and retiring to Mary King's previous Belsize villa enabled her to manage such an event discreetly.

55. *Gin Lane* (engraved by H. Adlard) by William Hogarth, 1751, later hand colour. Two prints published in support of what would become the Gin Act of 1751. The spire of St. George's, Bloomsbury in clearly visible in the background.

The two Hogarth prints reproduced here were published as a pair, to be viewed together. They contrast the evils of the consumption of gin ('mother's ruin') with the merits of drinking beer. The foreground and middle ground of the *Gin Lane* print portray the fate of drink befuddled prostitutes' children. Many of these abandoned babies were taken to the Foundling Hospital, of which Hogarth was a founding governor and which backed onto the graveyard of the two churches of St. George.

54. The companion print, *Beer Street* (engraved by S. Davenport) by William Hogarth, later hand colour. This scene is set in the parish of St. Martin-in-the-Fields and depicts the celebration of the birthday of King George II.

Did Hogarth wish to make a connection between the Gin Lane picture and the Foundling Hospital? The question is worth asking because Hogarth had organised a lottery of 2000 tickets for one of his paintings and sold around 1830 of them, with the remaining tickets given to the Foundling Hospital. The prize was his 1750 famous painting, *The March of the Guards to Finchley* (figures 58-61). Quite by happy coincidence the winning ticket was drawn by the Foundling Hospital!

56. *The Foundling Hospital,* Holborn, engraving with original hand colour by T. Bowles after Louis-Philippe Boitard, 1753, the Wellcome Collection, CC-BY 4.0.

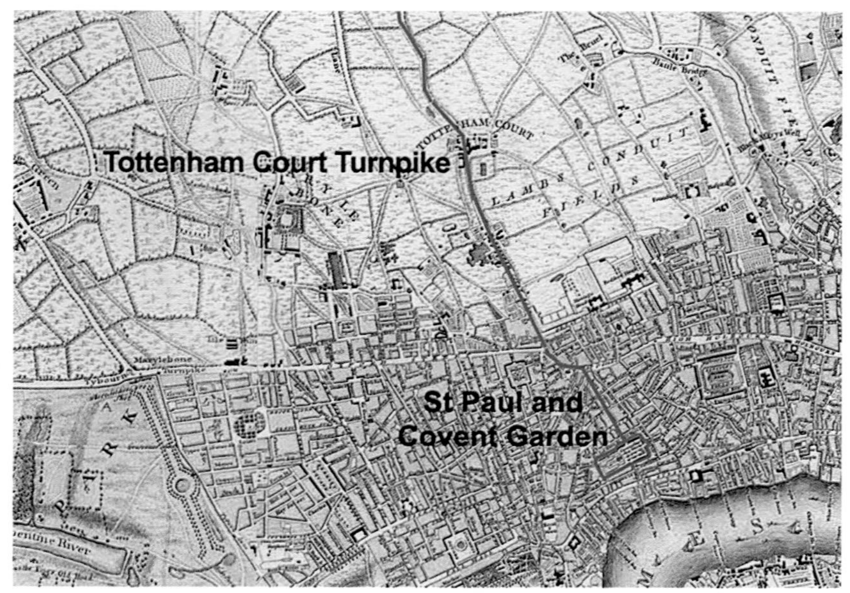

57. The route north from Covent Garden via Tottenham Court (and onwards to Hampstead) marked on John Rocque's London map of 1746.

58. *The March of the Guards to Finchley*, background detail, William Hogarth, *c.*1750, the Foundling Museum. According to Thomas Barratt in his *Annals of Hampstead,* Steele's cottage and Moll King's house[s] can be seen in the background of this picture.
Art Historian Dan Cruickshank asserts that 'in the distance, on the line of the march, lurks the residence of the woman many considered to have done much to undermine the morals of London.'

Some authors have identified the buildings depicted in the distant background of *The March of the Guards to Finchley* as Haverstock Hill and Hampstead. This route includes Steele's Cottage which featured in an edition of *The Monthly Magazine.* In issue No.6 of Volume 56, dated January 1, 1824 it reported:

> In Hogarth's 'March to Finchley,' this cottage and Mother King's House are seen in the distance; and the last occupant a very aged milkman, told the writer that he well remembered this famous march by his cottage, the men being mostly drunk, in great disorder, and accompanied by hundreds of trulls (harlots).

59. *The March of the Guards to Finchley*, full image, William Hogarth, *c.*1750, the Foundling Museum. Here you can see the orderly row of soldiers leaving London. Featuring the English guards setting out to protect the capital from the second Jacobite Rebellion of 1745, led by Bonnie Prince Charlie. Hogarth's reason for including the distant houses – some of which owned by a woman who made her fortune from prostitution – is no doubt confirmed by the insertion of a brothel in the right foreground.

60. *The March of the Guards to Finchley*, detail, William Hogarth, *c.*1750. Some harlots are also depicted down among the soldiers plying their trade.

61. Mother Douglas's brothel in *The March of the Guards to Finchley,* detail, William Hogarth, *c.*1750. With Mother Douglas herself ('Empress o'er all the bawds around') in the window at bottom right. The Douglas' girls display themselves at each window, while the cats on the roof confirm the house is a 'cattery'.

Surely here, in typical Hogarthian style, is the use of creative licence that intentionally introduced Mother Douglas's brothel (transported from its actual location in Covent Garden) into a scene set at the location of the Tottenham Court Turnpike, while at the same time emphasising the link between the Covent Garden bawdy-houses and Hampstead's bawdy-houses.

If all that was not enough connection, the land appropriated for the creation of St. George's Bloomsbury originally formed part of the parish of St. Giles-in-the-Fields, which Mary Hoff's will cited as recipient of her estates if her child Charles should die without heirs. Built by Hawksmoor between 1716 and 1731 the church was rising during the years that saw the parallel rise of Tom and Mary King in Covent Garden's coffee-house scene.

The conflation of the coffee-house culture with the procuration and usage of females for prostitution to the well to do, and the twin ravages of unprotected sex and drink, resulted in thousands of unwanted and orphaned children. Thomas Coram's well-intentioned Foundling Hospital soon became swamped by this tide of sadness, despite the best efforts of Hogarth and the other founder governors. Many of Hogarth's paintings repeat these themes from the various points of view of the different participants.

Which brings us to how Nancy Dawson would have ended up in Mary's Haverstock Hill villa.

By her own account Mary's only son was Charles. While there is no record for a Charles being christened in St. Paul's Covent Garden, there is one in the baptismal register for a Charles King born on July 14 and christened on August 4, 1728 in St. Martin-in-the-Fields. So it really does look as if this 'only son' of Mary's was born out of wedlock, during her 'time off from Tom'.

August
1 Francis Barker Devaynes of John & Mary — Jul 3
1 Catherine Shorter of William & Catherine — Jul 30
3 Charlotte Cope of Charles & Frances — Jul 23
4 Mary Ewins of John & Mary — Jul 21
4 John Acton of James & Mary — Jul 28
4 Charles King of Thomas & Mary — Jul 14
4 Isabella Downes of Edward & Sarah — Jul 21
4 John Gascoyne of William & Anne — Jul 13
4 Samuel Hinchley of John & Sarah — Aug 4
4 John Kemp of John & Anne — Aug 4

62. Baptism records of St. Martin-in-the-Fields for August 1728.

That being said, in those days if Tom was the male protector of his 'Moll' Mary, their 'wedding' officiated by a defrocked priest, rather infers that this was perhaps a union in name only. The fact that her second wedding to Hoff was actually held in a church rather underscores this hypothesis concerning Tom King. And belatedly one notes that Mary's cordwainer father was not necessarily the poor or neglectful man alluded to in the stories of Mary. He may have had to work hard but he was a qualified shoemaker and, as a chamber master, had his own shoe shop.

63. A cordwainer or shoemaker.

Both Mary and Tom it seems, in selecting their profession of coffee-house-cum-bawdy-house keepers, fell from the grace of their respective fathers.

So we have Charles King accepted into the 'household' already established by Tom and his wife and then we have 'a pupil of Mary's', who turns out to be another child of the same age, Ann Newton. It follows that these two children would have known each other in their formative years. Charles inherited his mother's estate on reaching the age of 30 in 1758, five years before Ann, now Nancy Dawson, would move to the villa, and whether or not their childhood bond remained simply that or it had become more, Charles was certainly able to provide a refuge for her. Thomas Barratt in *The Annals of Hampstead* assumed that 'Nancy was probably attracted to Haverstock Hill by a desire to be near her old dancing mistress, Moll King. It was in a neat little villa close by these, and not far from Steele's cottage, that Nancy took her ease in her later years.' This is a bit of a flimsy assumption, since Mary King had already been dead for sixteen years. In an edition of *The Monthly Magazine* edited by John Aikin, Sir Richard Phillips had written, 'Mother or Moll King built three substantial houses; and in a small villa behind them resided her favourite pupil, Nancy Dawson.' But this edition of the magazine was published in 1824 – over sixty years after the demise of Moll and the records of Nancy Dawson's later occupation of the villa.

In her will Nancy left virtually all her worldly goods to her parents, her brother William and his wife. This might be a belated attempt to reconnect with her family and an attempt to compensate for the disappointment that her choice of profession (with its commonly believed association with prostitution) might have been to her family. There is no evidence that it succeeded, and the only remaining memorial of Nancy is in Belsize.

Dawson Terrace, Nos. 72-80 Haverstock Hill – incorporating a redeveloped No. 80 – now continues on down the hill from 'Moll King's Row' with the date of the terrace's construction, 1882, still clearly visible on the parapet.

64. Plaque marking Dawson Terrace, Haverstock Hill built 1882.

64a. Dawson Terrace, Nos.72-80 Haverstock Hill; more about this terrace in the next chapter.

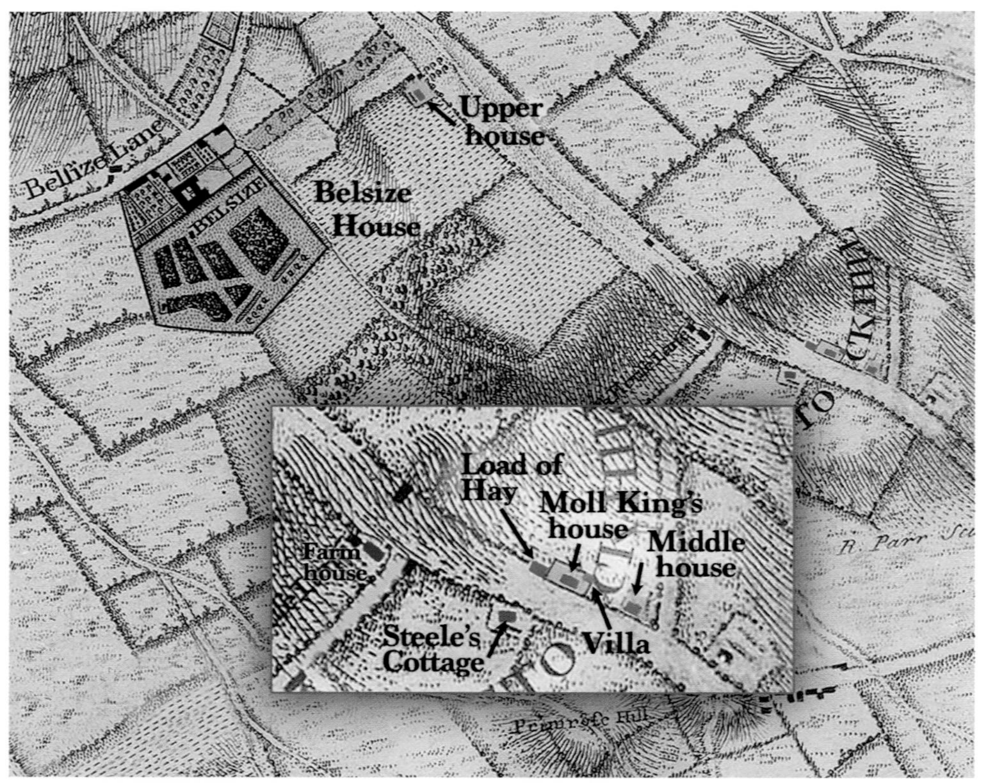

65. Probable location of Moll's houses marked in red and annotated on the section of John Rocque's 1746 sixteen-sheet London map covering the Haverstock Hill area.
The building by the lane leading south west was the farmhouse occupied by a Mr. T. Stringfield in 1714 – its location was on the corner of Upper Chalk House Lane, now called England's Lane.

CHAPTER 7

Remaining traces of Moll King

By great good fortune, John Rocque was surveying London and its environs just at the time when Mary and Tom King were acquiring property on Haverstock Hill. Roque's sixteen-sheet, exquisitely detailed map was published in 1746.

On the section of the map where the words HAVERSTOCK HILL appear, one house is shown on the western side of the highway, which indisputably represents Steele's cottage, and three buildings directly across the road from it. On the enlarged portion of the map shown in figure 65 I have labelled what I believe them to represent: the *Load of Hay* (a pub bearing that name until recently still stands there), Mary's house and Tom's 'middle house', so named in his will.

Supporting these hypotheses is the early engraving (figure 36, p.58) which shows Tom King's (later, Mary's) timber-famed house as standing solitary by the eastern side of the highway, with only a single cottage between it and the city of London in the distance.

18th-century records show that only three new houses were built on the Belsize estate between 1714 and 1750. Some scholars, arguing from the known proximity of Mary King's house to Steele's cottage and the present-day site of Steele's Road and Mews and the Sir Richard Steele public house, wrongly located Mary's three houses at Nos. 82-84 Haverstock Hill directly across the highway from there, and referred to them as 'Moll King's Row'. It is my contention that Moll never owned a row, but two houses as shown by Rocque plus one further up the hill at the junction of a path leading to Belsize House. This third building I believe was Tom's (later Mary's) Upper House, which was either owned or rented, and significantly conveniently close to the workplace for Mary's girls.

Rocque's map shows one more building, placed behind Mary's main house away from the road. Significantly, this building lies within the rectangular boundary of the main house. This must be the villa identified by many sources as the retreat of Nancy Dawson, who thus remained under the wing and protection of Mary King even after the latter's death.

The first record of the building on the 'upper house' site (where Hillfield Court now stands) appeared around 1646. It was known at that time as the Blue House. Accessed directly from Haverstock Hill, it was one of the rural residences in the Belsize area belonging to wealthy merchants – an ideal location for a country residence easily reached from London. Although little is on record concerning the residents, research reveals that in 1679 the property was occupied by a Thomas Butler. The house was later rebuilt with stabling by the under-tenant William Horseley between the years 1761 and 1773.

Given the secrecy surrounding Mary King's business dealings, it is difficult to be certain how the houses were used. Taking the business model of King's Coffee House, the working girls would have been totally separate from the King's own Tudor-style home, operating from two bawdy-houses, the middle house adjacent to Mary King's own house and the Blue House site. This middle house was ideally located for clients other than those from Belsize House – servicing *The Load of Hay* customers as well as the Chalcot area and Primrose Hill. One can speculate that after the death of her second husband John, as time went on, Mary might have moved into the small villa, thereby expanding the business into her large timber-framed building, but what appears certain is that she always followed her own dictum of living separately from the business.

Today the word 'villa' can refer to various types and sizes of residences, from the suburban semi-detached double or paired villa, to an urban property, but the term was first adopted by the English in the early 18th century, when it was applied to compact houses in the country, especially those which were accessible from London.

In the early 1800s, fifty years after Mary's death, London's outer villages were turning into suburbs and it is highly likely that, for reasons of space as well as the outdated part-timber construction, most of Mary's properties would have been demolished and the gardens parcelled up. Mary's house may have burned down even earlier. In any case, by the late 18th century nobody of any social pretensions would have wanted to live in such an old-fashioned house so close to London.

66. Detail from *Steele's Cottage Haverstock Hill,* from an original study by William Westall, engraved by Edward Finden, 1829. The original *Load of Hay* tavern is marked. The tall houses fronting the hill have survived. Notice the **three-window arrangement** on the top floors of the farther of the two taller houses (closer view in figure 69 below). The candidate for the villa is on the right. The original footprint of the middle house was probably near to where the tall green conifer is depicted.

The houses in this 1829 engraving of Haverstock Hill appear to be a development of narrow London-type plots including a semi-detached pair adjacent to *The Load of Hay.* The properties to the right of them are typical of early 19th-century ribbon development.

But what exactly is the tall building on the right – was this the 'small villa' referred to by Sir Richard Phillips in his *Monthly Magazine* and in the anonymously authored *The Life and Character of 'Moll' King*? (see the Sources). I decided to take a closer, detailed look at the architecture. This tall, rectangular building is shown set back from the road and slightly further down the hill in a location which matches that shown on John Rocque's 1746 map.

The building is also included on maps and plans of London and its vicinity published in 1824, 1837 and 1862. The villa is shown as being almost as tall as the houses fronting the road and featuring a loggia – a covered exterior gallery on the south-eastern side. The villa appears artificially elevated, drawn taller than in reality. This may well be an application of artistic licence, a rather clever way for the artist, William Westall, to include the villa in the engraving. Such cheating enables it to be seen, in the correct location; without it, the building would not be visible as it was situated behind the houses fronting the hill. This 'false elevation' hypothesis is supported by the fact that in this engraving, no fenestration is depicted below the two visible floors.

The two buildings with the unique fenestration shown in the 1829 engraving appear at this location a few doors south of *The Load of Hay* in the 2018 photograph and are present-day Nos. 82 and 84 Haverstock Hill. These were clearly of much later construction than Mary's house, although they are indeed on the same site. These houses have for decades been incorrectly called 'Moll King's Row'. As late as 2006 historians mistakenly concluded that 'these are clearly two of the three houses built by Moll King' and hence perpetuated the belief that Moll built a row of houses for herself in the 1730s. I hope that I have now dispelled this illusion.

Contemporary records describe a 'small villa' behind the main house. The building with the loggia now becomes a candidate for that villa, despite its apparent height, because it is precisely on the site indicated by John Rocque's map.

67. The rebuilt 1863 *Load of Hay* in 2018 with terraced houses and shops on the eastern side of Haverstock Hill extending down the hill to the south.

68. This terrace today has retail shops at street level and of particular note is the unusual **three-window arrangement** of the upper floor of the circled pair of buildings (compare with figure 69). The slightly shorter building, now No. 80, was rebuilt almost a century later as part of Dawson Terrace.

69. Detail from the 1829 engraving emphasising the three-window arrangement on the furthest upper two floors (compare with figure 68).

No longer town houses as such, they now have shop premises at street level with flats above. It would be reasonable to conclude that these terraced houses, which became known as 'Moll King's Row', were constructed on what was once land belonging to Tom and Mary King – and that the buildings, albeit now partly redeveloped, are those depicted in the 1829 Haverstock Hill engraving. No. 82 Haverstock Hill, now with a ground floor bar and restaurant known as the Tupelo Honey boasts, with some justification, a distant relationship with the properties of Mary 'Moll' King.

Is there any further evidence that these properties were replacements of what has now been identified as Moll King's houses?

There is, but it's rather gruesome. Inevitably, at any one time during the course of their work, a number of Mary's working girls would become pregnant despite, in some cases, going to extreme lengths to avoid such an outcome. Various methods were available in those days to try to dispose of pregnancies, including 'Old Uncle Henry' the herb Mugwort, but they were not without

70. The welcoming Tupelo Honey bar and restaurant, photo: Tupelo Honey.

their dangers and they generally resulted in poor success rates. Failure to terminate meant the mother-to-be had to choose whether she wanted to allow her baby to live – no doubt a painful and difficult choice. It is known, but only from a confidential source familiar with the grounds of the present low-built villa on that site, that several small skeletons had been found buried in the land just beyond the house and villa. This land is shown on several later maps and was known as 'Moll King's Field'.

This is perhaps ironic given young Tom King's 'orphan' burial in St. Paul's churchyard. He might well have been fathered by Tom senior with one of Mary's girls, so an option might have been to bury him in the field, but that would undoubtedly have been too close to their home and far too much to bear.

In what seems to be a strange twist of fate, some years later this land would become the site of the Orphan Working School. The school was originally established in Hoxton before it moved in 1847 to occupy the northern part of Moll King's Field, the entrance being from the road named Maitland Park Villas.

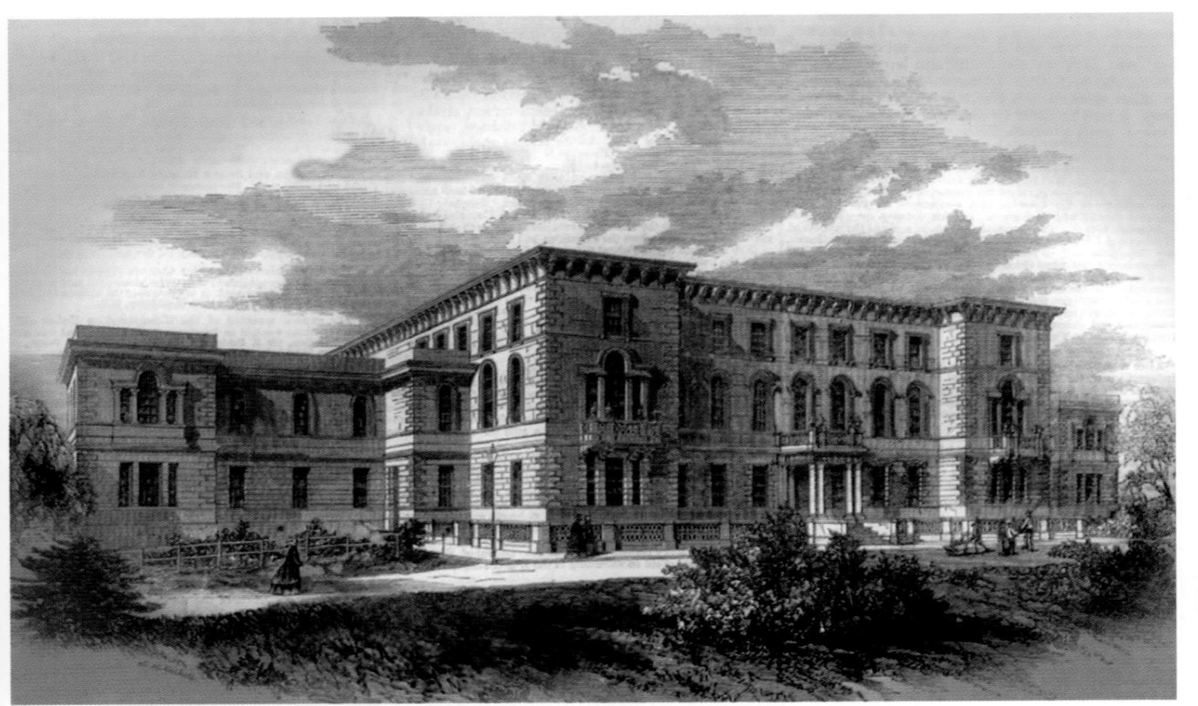

71. The Orphan Working School in 1861, wood engraved print from the *Illustrated London News*. The school moved to Maitland Park off Haverstock Hill, and was built on Moll King's Field, shortly after acquisition of the land in 1847, 100 years after Mary Hoff's death. Subsequent development of the site has left only a pair of distinctive gate piers.

Here, orphans and other needy children were clothed, educated and wholly maintained. About 420 children were in the school and they were known by numbers rather than their names. At fourteen, the boys were apprenticed, while the girls remained for a year or two longer, training for domestic service. Years later the school was demolished and the site subsequently developed. All that remains are two pairs of the school's distinctive gate piers, now moved to two different locations, gracing an apartment block and the Maitland Park Care Home.

Coming back to the villa, a modest building can be seen to this day from the grounds of the care home on exactly the square site behind present No.80 that is marked on Rocque's and all subsequent maps of the area.

Reassuringly, a strong candidate (although more cottage than villa) still exists on the site. Modern maps show a building occupying the same virtually square footprint within the same land boundaries.

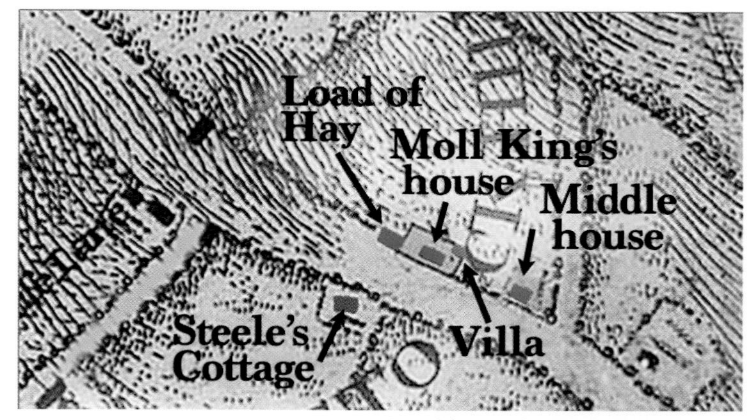

72. Detail from John Rocque's 1746 map.

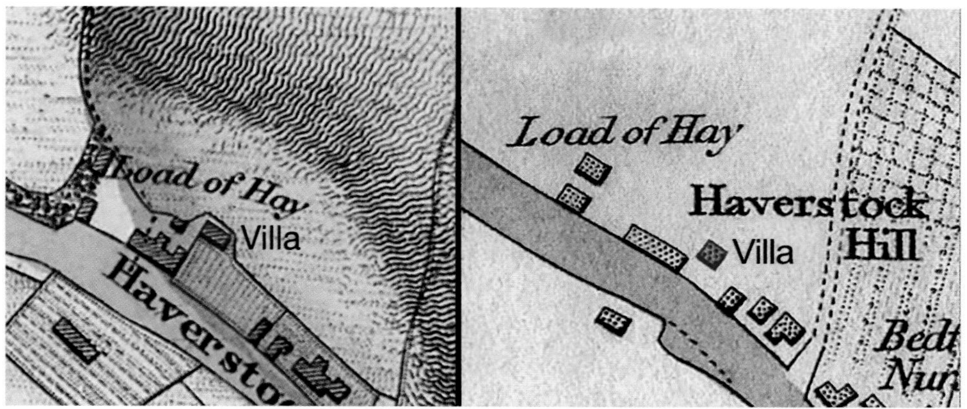

73. Left: Greenwood's 1824 map, and Right: Cary's 1837 map suggesting that the villa is consistently present – *The Load of Hay* is marked in blue, the villa is highlighted in red.

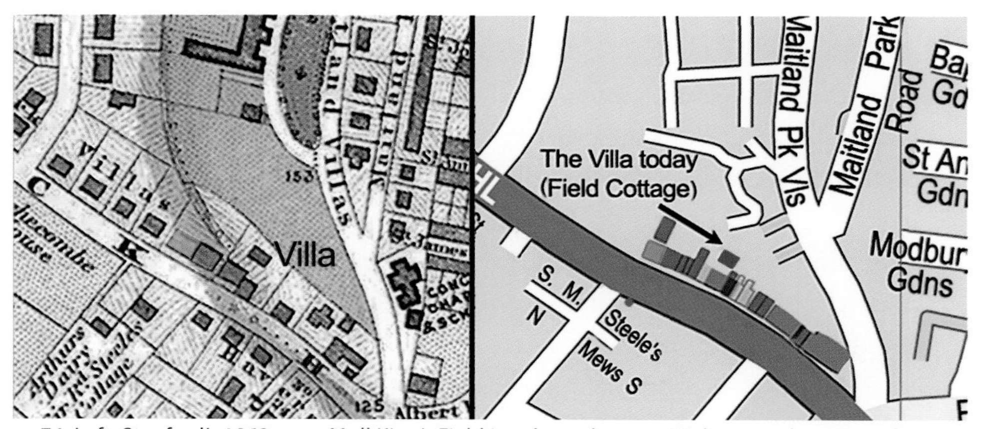

74. Left: Stanford's 1862 map, Moll King's Field is coloured green. Right: a modern map, the position of the villa is virtually unchanged. The old footpath slightly further down the hill is now Maitland Park Villas.

75. Haverstock Hill, © Crown copyright 2020 OS licence No. 100062516, with added blue for the pub and red for the villa. As far as can be reasonably determined the villa or cottage remaining today occupies the same footprint as did Mary King's original villa. A milestone (see figures 83 & 84) is marked in blue.

I contacted the local estate agent Naylius McKenzie at No. 74 Haverstock Hill and learned that this small villa, set behind the present day terrace of houses and shops is now called Field Cottage. I then got in touch with the owner of the ground floor apartment, Amit Shah, who kindly allowed me to visit and take pictures. The property is accessed from Haverstock Hill via a doorway in the terrace, leading to a passageway. On exiting through a rear door, the area opens up into a small courtyard on the south-western side of the property. Each of the other three sides has a paved area with retaining brick walls (here topped with trellis) designed to hold back the higher ground beyond and thus protect the lower floor of the villa.

Unfortunately, but not unsurprisingly, over the years the building has undergone many changes and adjustments. The interiors have been updated and few of the original features have survived.

Has any other confirmatory evidence of the existence of these properties survived? Yes – there is Tom King's will which provides an inventory of some of the contents of their properties. And there is Mary's will, both in the National Archives.

76. Field Cottage in the spring of 2018, seen from the east.
The groundsman responsible for the upkeep of the land surrounding Field Cottage states that the green area in the foreground was once a vegetable garden.

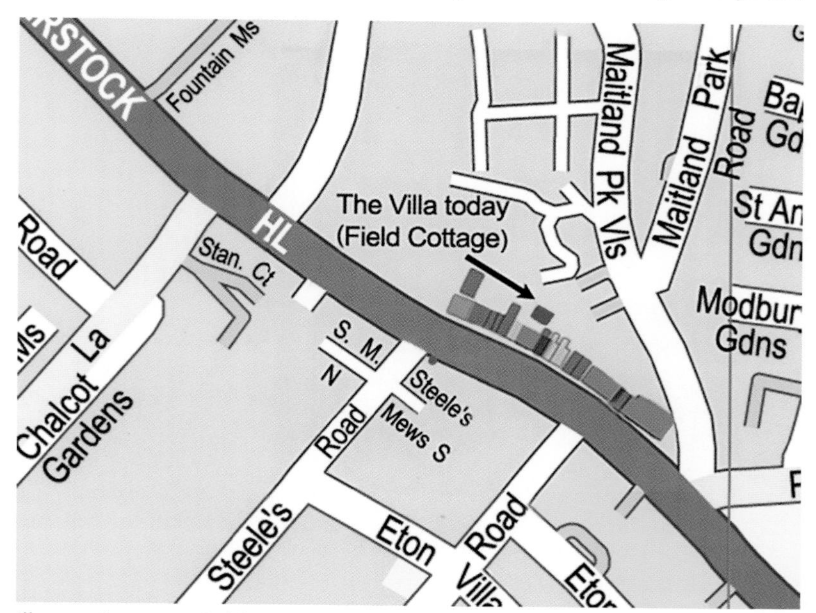

77. The villa, now known as Field Cottage on a modern street map (larger image). Note the milestone (blue dot) on the corner of Steele's Road, opposite *The Load of Hay,* see figures 83 & 84.

78. Courtyard on the south-western side of the building running parallel with Haverstock Hill.

79. South-eastern aspect where the loggia would have been located, as depicted in figure 66. Part of the rear elevation of the Haverstock Hill yellow brick terrace is in the background.

80. North-western side of the building – part of the retaining wall is on the left and at the rear.

81. North-western side of the cottage as seen from the field beyond the property showing a relatively new mansard-style roof with Velux windows.

Mary's will is under her second married name, Hoff, which clearly states that she owned copyhold and leasehold properties in Hampstead, Covent Garden and Soho. Although the *Load of Hay* tavern was in Hampstead, Mary Hoff's land and houses were actually in the adjoining manor (which became part of the Parish of St. Pancras) as can been seen on a 1790 map (green area, figure 83).

In fact one of Mary's transactions has been traced referring to 'all the close of land containing by estimation nine acres... in the occupation of the said Mary Hoffe'. This matter is the subject of a Tottenham (or Tottenhall) Special Court Baron dated November 19, 1746.

There is something else of interest that has survived from Mary Hoff's time. It is not a building, but a milestone marker (see figures 83 & 84).

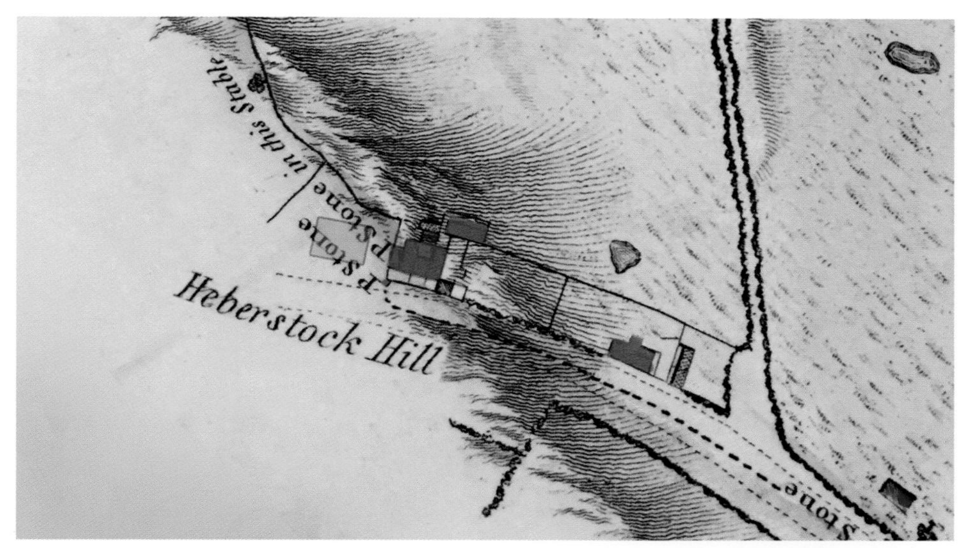

83. Part of the 1790 map of the Parish of St. Pancras in the county of Middlesex, from a survey by J. Thompson, British Library. Here the map has been rotated to show north at the top. Mary King's houses and the villa are highlighted in red. Note the boundary line that excludes *The Load of Hay* next door (marked pale blue) – not included on the original map as it stood in the Manor of Hampstead, south of the yellow boundary. The area in green is the Tottenhall side. The original milestone (marked P. Stone, blue dot) was located by *The Load of Hay.* At some point, probably when Mary King's houses were rebuilt, the stone was moved 45 feet to the other side of Haverstock Hill opposite *The Load of Hay.*

84. The milestone today, moved from its original location on the opposite side of the road, and repositioned on the corner of Steele's Road. It reads: '**4 Miles from the Post Office**'. The first general post office in London was located in the City and opened in 1643 eight years after King Charles I legalised use of the royal posts for private correspondence. The inscription at the bottom of the stone: '**45ft North**' refers to the stone's repositioning from its original location.

85. Crown Lodge, Haverstock Hill.

Further up Haverstock Hill, No.148, known as Crown Lodge has its origin in 1761 and is currently regarded as one of the oldest surviving houses in Belsize Park. As today's Belsize Park includes what was Mary King's land, perhaps we should now include her villa, Field Cottage, with its origins in the 1730s as the earliest recorded property in Belsize Park.

This chronicle is one of many that accounts for how the sex trade contributed to property building and acquisition in the expanding London of the mid 18th century.

Moll King's Coffee House survived Mary and it is mentioned in the *Adventures of Roderick Random* (1748) with the coffee-house described as a 'kind of brothel'.

We may never know for certain the full details of Mary King's complex life that ended on Haverstock Hill all those years ago, but her story, reprehensible though many aspects might be, is also that of a true survivor and entrepreneur.

A Sketch from Nature, William Paulet Carey, 1784, detail, the Met Collection, Metropolitan Museum of Art, New York.

Sources

Aitken, G. A. (Introduction and notes) *Richard Steele* (London, T. Fisher Unwin, Paternoster Square, 1894).

Anon., *The New Cheats of London Exposed; Or, the Frauds and Tricks of the Town Laid Open to Both Sexes* (London, 1792).

Anon., *Nocturnal Revels, the history of King's-place, and other modern nunneries* (London, 1779).

Anon., *The Life and Character of Moll King: Late Mistress of King's Coffee-house in Covent-Garden, who Departed this Life at Her Country-House at Hampstead, on Thursday the 17th of September, 1747. Containing A True Narrative of this Well-known Lady, from Her Birth to Her Death.* (London, W. Price, near the Sessions-House in the Old Baily, 1747).

Anon., *Memoirs of the Shakespear's-Head in Covent Garden: In which are introduced many entertaining adventures, and several remarkable characters* (London, 1755).

Anon., *Tom King's Or the Phabian Grove, With The Humours of Covent Garden, The Theatre, Gaming Table, Etc.* (London, 1738).

Anon., *Covent Garden in Mourning* (London, 1747).

Ellis, Aytoun, *The Penny Universities: A history of the coffee-houses* (London, Secker & Warburg, 1956).

Baker, Thomas, *Hampstead Heath: A Comedy As it was Acted at the Theatre Royal in Drury Lane By the author of The yeoman of Kent,* act II, scene 1. A revised version of the banned *An Act at Oxford: A Comedy* by Thomas Baker (London, printed for Bernard Lintott, 1706).

Barker, G. F. Russell, and Stenning, lan H. (Compiled) *The Record of Old Westminsters: All former pupils from the earliest times to 1927* (London, Chiswick Press, 1928).

Barratt, Thomas J. *The Annals of Hampstead* in three volumes (London, Adam and Charles Black Ltd., 1912).

Bindman, David, *Hogarth and his Times* (London, Brit. Museum Press, 1997).
Camden History Society, *The Streets of Gospel Oak* (London, 2006).
Dobson, Austin, *Eighteenth Century Vignettes* (London, Thomas Nelson and Son, 1892).
Eger, Elizabeth and Grant, Charlotte (Ed.) *Women and the Public Sphere, writing and representation, 1700-1830*. Part one, Markman Ellis, "The coffee-women, *The Spectator* and the public sphere in the early eighteenth century" (Cambridge University Press, 2001).
Forrester, Harry, *The Timber-Framed Houses of Essex* (Chelmsford, The Tindal Press, 1959).
Goadby, M., *Nocturnal Revels: Or, the History of King's-Place and Other Modern Nunneries with the portraits of the most celebrated DemiReps and Courtezans of this Period* (London, Paternoster Row, 1779).
Harwood Thomas, *Alumni Etonenses: Or A catalogue of the provosts & fellows of Eton College & King's College, Cambridge, from the foundation in 1443 to the year 1797* (Birmingham, 1797).
Highfill, Philip H, Burnim, Kalman A., Langhans, E., *A Biographical Dictionary of Actors, Actresses, etc* 1660-1800 (USA, SIU Press, 1984).
Hilliard, Anthony, *A Brief and Merrie History of England*, pamphlet guidebook (London, 1730).
Howitt, William, *The Northern Heights of London* (London, Longman, Green, and Co., 1869).
Lillywhite, Byrant, *London Coffee Houses: a reference book of coffee houses of the seventeenth, eighteenth and nineteenth centuries* (London, George Allen and Unwin, 1963).
Park, John James, *The Topography and Natural History of Hampstead in the County of Middlesex* (London, printed for White, Cochrane, and Co., Fleet Street; and Nichols, Son, and Bentley, Red Lion Passage, 1814).
Phillips, Richard, (Founder) Aikin, John (Ed.) *The Monthly Magazine* (London, published from February 1796).
Shelley, Henry C., *Inns and Taverns of Old London* (Boston, L. C. Page & Company, 1909).
Slater, H. and Adams, R., *The Tricks of the Town Laid Open: Or, a Companion for Country Gentlemen: Being the Substance of Seventeen Letters from a Gentleman in London to His Friend in the Country* (London, 1746).
Smollett, Tobias, *The Adventures of Roderick Random,* in two volumes (London, for J. Osborn, Paternoster Row, 1748).

Thompson, F.M.L., *Hampstead: Building a Borough* (London, Routledge & Kegan Paul Books, 1974).

Timbs, John, *Club Life of London: With Anecdotes of the Clubs, Coffee-Houses and Taverns of the Metropolis during the 17th, 18th, and 19th Centuries,* in two volumes (London, Richard Bentley, New Burlington Street, 1866).

Wade, Christopher (Author), Woodford, F. Peter (Ed.) *More Streets of Hampstead* (London, Camden History Society, 1973).

Walford, Edward, *Old and New London: A Narrative of its History, its People, its Places,* Volume 5, (London, Cassell, Petter & Galpin, 1873).

Wrigley, E. A., Schofield, Roger S., *The Population History of England, 1541-1871* (London, Edward Arnold (Publishers) Ltd., 1981).

Wyndham, Henry Saxe, *The Annals of Covent Garden Theatre from 1732 to 1897* (London, Chatto & Windus, 1906).

Alexander Prize Lecture, The, "Rethinking Politeness in Eighteenth-Century England: Moll King's Coffee House," Transactions of the Royal Historical Society Vol.11, (Cambridge University Press, 2001).

British History Online, primary and secondary sources for the history of Britain and Ireland, focusing on the years 1300 and 1800, www.british-history.ac.uk

Eton College Archives, Collections Administrator, Eton College Collections, Windsor.

Registers of St. Paul's Church, Covent Garden, London.

"Garrick Club Records", accessed September, 2018, www.garrick.ssl.co.uk.

"Hillfield Court Site History", accessed May 2018, en.wikipedia.org/wiki/Hillfield_Court.

"List of Tenants, Belsize Subordinate Manor," Westminster Abbey Library.

"London Lives, 1690-1800", accessed September 2018, www.londonlives.org.

"Nancy Dawson", the tune played by Sara & Maynard Johnson with Rogues' Consort, 1999, www.youtube.com/watch?v=T5LJZgYHaI0.

New York Public Library digital collections, https://picryl.com.

Will of John Hoff, Carpenter of Saint Anne, Westminster, Middlesex, The National Archives, Kew, Richmond, Surrey.

Will of Mary Hoff, Widow of Saint Paul, Covent Garden, Middlesex, The National Archives, Kew, Richmond, Surrey.

Will of Thomas King of Saint Paul, Covent Garden, Middlesex, The National Archives, Kew, Richmond, Surrey.

Acknowledgements

It's been tremendous fun putting this book together, but it would not have been possible without the initial push that helped to get it all underway. Aileen Hammond, a resident of Belsize Park, first drew my attention to the short terrace of houses on Haverstock Hill known locally as Moll King's Row, with its unusual fenestration, and this prompted my initial research into their history. And I am really glad she did so.

But where to start? It was another Belsize resident, F. Peter Woodford, who cajoled and spurred on the initial development of the story. Peter thought at first it might be an article but as time passed, when the scope of the story expanded, it became clear the text was too long for that. By the time the pictures were added the story evolved into these 120 or so pages. Peter's continued enthusiasm, invaluable assistance, expert guidance and encouragement have been absolutely invaluable, keeping my nose to the historical grindstone. I thank him wholeheartedly for relentlessly checking historical statements and patiently unravelling syntactical tangles.

I am most grateful to my marvellous wife Frances Pinter for tolerating my spending so much time with so many ladies of 'ill repute'. Without question she permitted me to spend hours researching and writing on my trusty laptop when and wherever we went on holiday, returning cheerfully recounting the excursions and sights I'd missed. Over the years Frances' extensive experience has provided extremely helpful publishing guidance and invaluable advice.

It was essential to be able to visit Field Cottage, and I am most appreciative of the help and assistance provided by Amit Shah, owner of the ground floor apartment, who very kindly allowed access to the property.

Which brings me to recognise Charles Hind, the Chief Curator of the RIBA Architectural Library, London. I am most grateful to him for his specialist advice and the information he kindly provided on several occasions regarding what probably happened to the Haverstock Hill houses following the death of Mary King.

I also wish to include my appreciation for the kind help and assistance from Georgina Robinson, Archives Assistant at the Eton College Library, Eton College, and Charles Grant, Church Administrator and Concert Director of St. Paul's Church, Covent Garden.

My thanks and deep gratitude must go to my great friend and writing colleague Mary Bennett who aided the project considerably, providing valuable additional research and offering many constructive ideas that improved and shaped the construction. I fully appreciate the contribution made by Caroline Handley who was exceedingly helpful with editing and polishing the text.

And it all came together when art historian and specialist in Georgian London, Dan Cruickshank, so very kindly agreed to write the Foreword, to whom I offer my sincerest thanks.

Index

D

E

F

G

H

M

N

O

P

About the Author

avid S. Percy FRSA, ARPS was born and educated in London and is a long-standing resident of Belsize Park.

He is happily married with one wife, two children and three grandchildren. An internationally award-winning director and cinematographer, he has filmed from helicopters, the rear door of Hercules aircraft flying at 10,000 feet and out from the back of ambulances in the Middle East – travelling the world making documentaries visiting places like Nagaland in the foothills of the Himalayas.

Working with multi-national corporations as well as not-for-profit organisations and charities, Percy has also directed and photographed a number of films for cinema and TV. His first short movie *The Anna Contract* ran continuously in Leicester Square for three months in 1978 as the support for *The Stud,* starring Joan Collins.

His theatrical film credits also include *Knights Electric,* often referred to as an early precursor to the music video or pop promo. He photographed *The Third Dimension* in 1985, a major short film featuring the new Tornado aircraft produced for the British Ministry of Defence.

Percy directed and produced *The Belsize Story* in 2012, narrated by Fiona Bruce, an in-depth, feature-length film in two volumes of the history, architecture and people of Belsize Park. He also directed the documentary *Kohima: An Exploration of War, Memory and Gratitude,* Official Selection at the 8th Monaco Charity Film Festival, 2013.

Over the years his photographic work has been exhibited in galleries at home and abroad including the United Nations building in New York and in Burgh House, Hampstead.

Percy has authored and co-authored many articles, publications and books, co-compiling *Belsize Remembered,* a fully illustrated book with over 150 of his photographs. It features a collection of memories of the area, edited by F. Peter Woodford with a Foreword by Sir Derek Jacobi, becoming a local best seller. *Belsize Remembered* was first published in 2017 and immediately reprinted in 2018.

The BBC commissioned *Mindpower for Business,* a Mind Mapping training course on how to use the human brain more effectively, featuring internationally-acclaimed brain expert Tony Buzan. He also produced a popular Mind Mapping course for students, *Get Ahead and Ace your Exams.*

David Percy runs the Belsize Village website, belsizevillage.co.uk.

David S. Percy

Also from Aulis Publishers

BELSIZE Remembered

'This book is a delight. A small and perfectly formed masterpiece. It has an almost incredible cast of characters from Agatha Christie to Madame Zwingli: in between we meet Ben Nicholson, Freud, Jung, Thomas Mann, R D Laing, Henry Moore and Twiggy. A marvellous cluster of memories with lovely vignettes.'

Michael Wood, historian and BBC broadcaster

'This splendidly illustrated book of remembrances of Belsize provides ample evidence of a vibrant, handsome part of London. A feast of information and a visual delight.'

John Richardson, chairman, Camden History Society

The Belsize Story

The Belsize Story documentary film in two volumes is narrated by Belsize Park resident Fiona Bruce. Combining its fascinating historical background with a present-day architectural tour, this film records the evolution of Belsize Park right up to the present day, featuring its buildings, the settings and its people.

The films are free to stream online at **belsizevillage.co.uk**
Visit the **Belsize Village website** for news, photographs, events and information about Belsize Park at **belsizevillage.co.uk**

Belsize Park residents are welcome to join **The Belsize Society**
Contact **membership@belsize.org.uk**